ERICA WILSON'S NEEDLEPOINT

ADAPTED FROM OBJECTS IN THE COLLECTIONS OF

THE METROPOLITAN MUSEUM OF ART

ERICA WILSON'S NEEDLEPOINT

ADAPTED FROM OBJECTS IN THE COLLECTIONS OF

THE METROPOLITAN MUSEUM OF ART

BY

Erica Wilson

PHOTOGRAPHY BY

Randy O'Rourke

HARRY N. ABRAMS, INC., PUBLISHERS

Acknowledgments

Sincere acknowledgment is extended to the staff at the Metropolitan Museum, particularly Robie Rogge and Mary Beth Brewer. I would also like to thank my editor, Ellen Rosefsky Cohen, who has seen the book through with enthusiasm and perserverance, Carol Robson, for her dedication and creativity in designing the book, Randy O'Rourke, for his ingenious photography, needlepoint consultant Karyn Gerhard, Naomi Warner, my assistant Nichole Harris, and last but not least, my daughter Vanessa Diserio, who has been my right hand throughout the five-year project.

We thank Rakaam Magazine for their cooperation.

Dedication

To my husband, Vladimir Kagan,
my children, Jessica, Vanessa, and Illya,
and their children, Sandy, Mallory, and Olivia.

Editor: Ellen Rosefsky Cohen
Designer: Carol A. Robson
with Gilda Hannah

Title page: Quinces pillow with Berlin strip sampler (p. 53).

Library of Congress Cataloging-in-Publication Data

Wilson, Erica.
[Needlepoint]
    Erica Wilson's needlepoint : adapted from objects in the collections of the Metropolitan Museum of Art / by Erica Wilson ; photography by Randy O'Rourke.
        p. cm.
    ISBN 0–8109–3980–0
    1. Canvas embroidery—Patterns.   I. Title.
TT778.C3W563   1995
746.44′2—dc20   94–26890

Published in 1995 by Harry N. Abrams, Incorporated, New York
A Times Mirror Company

Printed and bound in Japan

Contents

Easy Chair (crewel back panel).
American (Newport, Mass.), 1758.

Spring Meadows

In 1950 Mrs. J. Insley Blair presented The Metropolitan Museum of Art a very special gift—a Queen Anne–style chair, dated 1758 and signed "Gardner Junr." Glowing with peacock blues and coral reds worked all over the front in a straight stitch repeat pattern known as Bargello, or flame stitch, the entire back of the chair is covered with a magnificent pastoral scene in crewel embroidery.

The design may have come from one of several needlework schools which were especially prevalent in New England in the eighteenth century. Americans often interpreted designs from European engravings by drawing them out on linen to be stitched.

Crewel embroidery at this time was generally used for bed curtains, valances, and soft coverings. The colonial embroiderers naturally used those materials close at hand—worsted wools and linen fabrics—to interpret in needlework their new world of deer, squirrels, peach orchards, wild grapes, and fields of watermelons and pumpkins.

Reducing the crewel design to a square needlepoint pillow is a definite challenge because the scale must be reduced without losing the essence of the colorful pattern. Since the design is a patchwork of individual scenes, almost any section would look charming used for different objects—a small zippered case or a child's chair, for instance. Or visualize the shepherd and his sheep as an eyeglass case, or the deer as the centerpiece for a pillow made larger with a "window frame" of velvet. The number of ways you can work with this pattern is endless. The needlepoint can be as striking and unusual today as when it was first created in crewel in the eighteenth century.

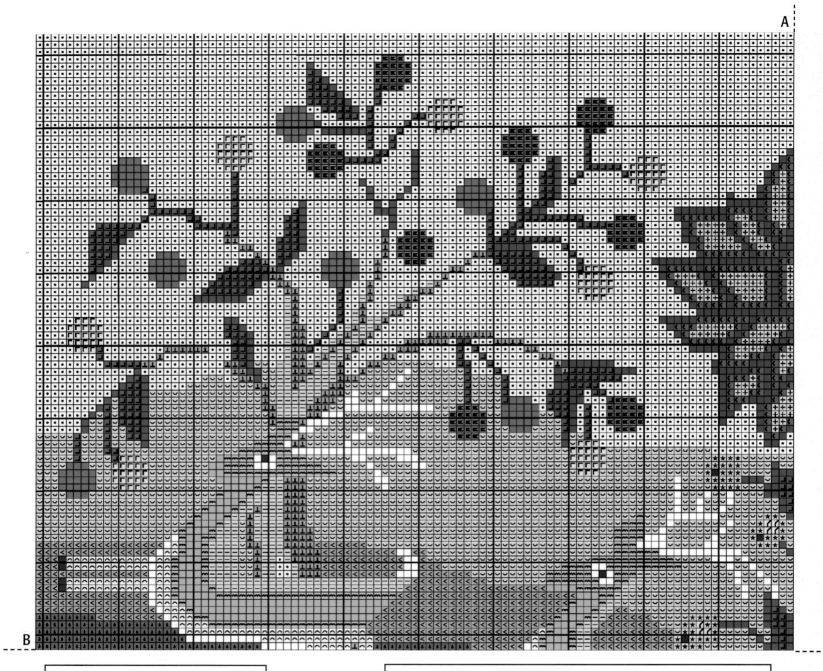

A

B

MATERIALS

14 mesh Mono canvas (cut size: 18 x 18")
Size 20 tapestry needle
24 shades Persian yarn (separate and use
   only 1 strand of 3-ply yarn)

201 stitches x 203 stitches

The design as shown was worked on 14
mesh canvas, using Erica Wilson Persian
yarn. To work on different sizes of mesh
with other yarns refer to the chart on p. 126.

Diagram for chart pp. 8–11:

<u>Note</u>: Using this diagram as a
guide, match up the letters and the
dotted lines showing where the
charts join. For instance, <u>A</u> is at the
edge of your first chart, marked
with a dotted line. On the second
chart, <u>A</u> is five stitches in from the
edge, also marked with a dotted
line. **This is a five-stitch repeat
which should not be worked**—it
is there to help you establish your
position when continuing on to
the next chart.

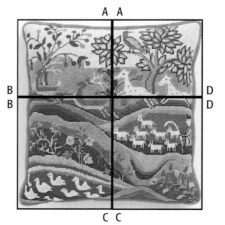

A A

B   D
B   D

C C

A

D

	Color #	Color (# of 3-ply 33" strands)
1.	EWP 1050	Black (2)
2.	EWP 5121	Dark Kelly Green (8)
3.	EWP 5122	Bright Kelly Green (8)
4.	EWP 5013	Medium Yellow Green (3)
5.	EWP 5063	Medium Misty Blue Green (14)
6.	EWP 5065	Light Misty Blue Green (14)
7.	EWP 5036	Light Yellow Green (18)
8.	EWP 7101	Very Dark Blue (10)
9.	EWP 7102	Dark Blue (10)
10.	EWP 7103	Medium Blue (10)
11.	EWP 7056	Pale Blue (6)
12.	EWP 1142	Dark Brown (4)
13.	EWP 4025	Medium Gold (6)
14.	EWP 4023	Dark Golden Rust (6)
15.	EWP 1145	Light Beige (3)
16.	EWP 1106	Medium Toast (8)
17.	EWP 3005	Light Apricot (10)
18.	EWP 1010	Cream (26)
19.	EWP 4072	Medium Orange (3)
20.	EWP 4014	Light Yellow (4)
21.	EWP 2061	Fushia (2)
22.	EWP 2064	Medium Pink (5)
23.	EWP 2047	Pale Pink (6)
24.	EWP 1001	White (8)

Elizabethan Embroidery

Embroidered Textile. English, early 17th century. Silk and metal thread on linen.
ROGERS FUND, 1934

The Elizabethan period was the golden age for embroidery in England. Increased luxury in household decoration meant that all the care, expertise, and rich materials that had formally gone into the creation of an altar frontal were now lavished upon a set of bed hangings or a padded "pillow bere" splendidly stitched with brilliant silks and gold threads. Every household had its resident embroiderer who was able to refurbish and make new embroideries for furnishings and costumes. "Pillow beres" were among the objects they would make. Useful as well as decorative, these little cushions must have certainly helped to soften the effect of sitting very straight on a hardwood seat in a stiff embroidered gown.

Similar to the pillows in design were the charming little "sweet bags." It was customary for members of the royal entourage to present the Queen with a gift every New Year's Day. If the gift was money, in the form of pieces of silver, it might be delivered in a small embroidered purse, or "sweet bag." Originally designed to disguise the mercenary nature of the gift, the sweet bags were so beautifully embroidered they became more valuable than the contents.

The most popular embroidered flowers of the period were the iris, carnation, marigold, rose, pomegranate, and the newly discovered tobacco plant recently brought back from the New World by Sir Walter Raleigh. Favorite designs were the diamond trellis or sweeping scrolls, each enclosing a colorful flower or fruit. Among these were often scattered pea pods, butterflies, caterpillars, and birds, all splendid in silks with real gold thread and spangles to give a glint of light here and there.

The textile from which the frame is adapted has all these flowers in crisp clean colors on ivory ground, with the metal thread now mellowed to an antique gold. The flowers, springing up between each intersection of the lattice, seem to have the prim freshness of an Elizabethan garden. The same pattern could also be worked out in a different scale using twelve mesh for a bench instead of the eighteen mesh for the frame shown here, or in fourteen mesh for a little purse.

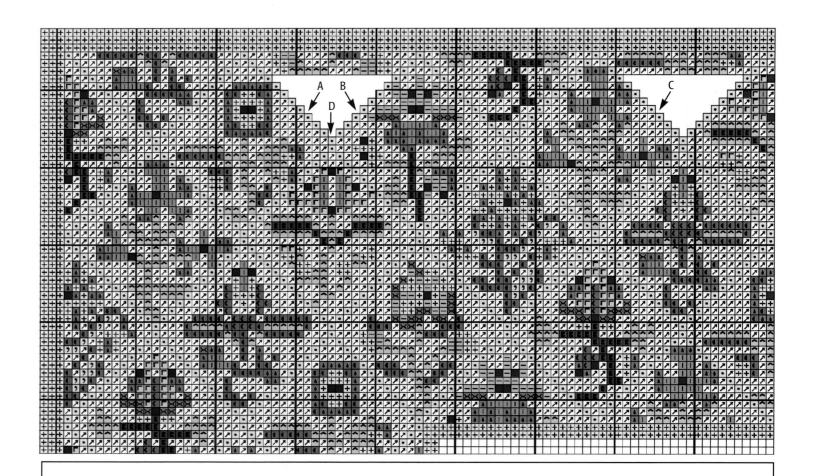

Note: The Elizabethan Embroidery Frame is made up of a pattern of 8 different flowers in a repeat pattern. The flowers are labeled A–H on the top of the chart. This chart represents a section of the frame, for color placement only. To make the whole frame, begin by stitching the diamond outlines and borders. Once your outline is completed, you can fill in the flowers; stitch the flowers in groups of 4: AGDB alternating with ECHF, using the diagram to the right as a guide. Also note that for this chart there is no 5-stitch repeat.

The photographs of the frame on pp. 12–13 differ slightly from the above chart. Follow the diagram for best results.

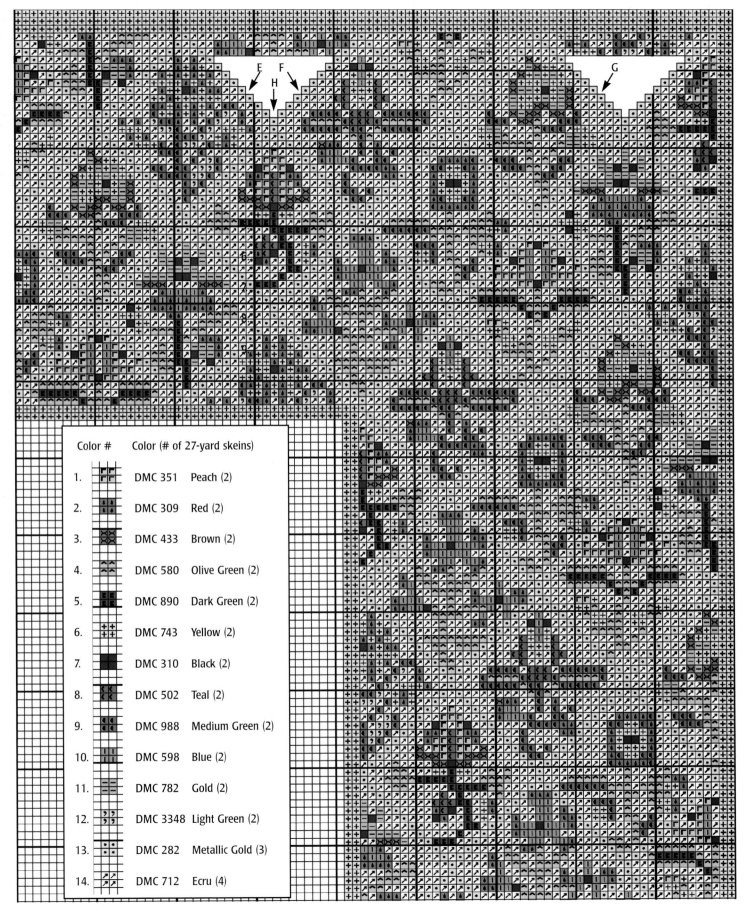

Color #		Color (# of 27-yard skeins)
1.		DMC 351 Peach (2)
2.		DMC 309 Red (2)
3.		DMC 433 Brown (2)
4.		DMC 580 Olive Green (2)
5.		DMC 890 Dark Green (2)
6.		DMC 743 Yellow (2)
7.		DMC 310 Black (2)
8.		DMC 502 Teal (2)
9.		DMC 988 Medium Green (2)
10.		DMC 598 Blue (2)
11.		DMC 782 Gold (2)
12.		DMC 3348 Light Green (2)
13.		DMC 282 Metallic Gold (3)
14.		DMC 712 Ecru (4)

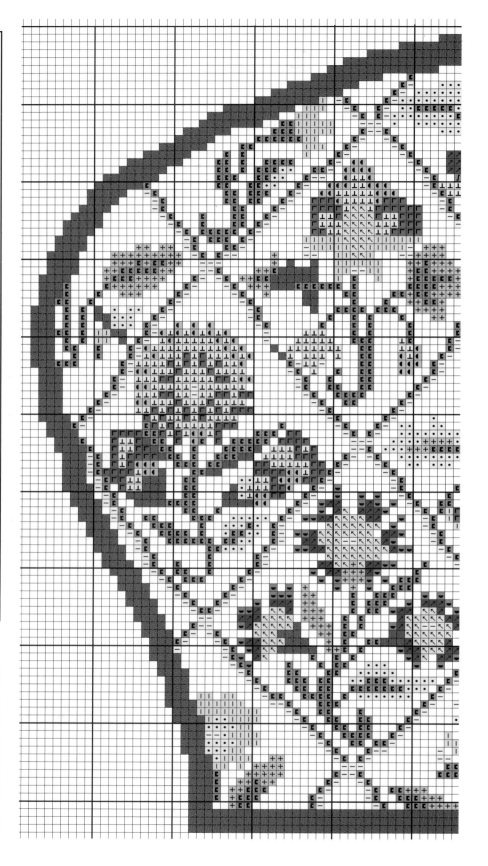

Color #	Color (# of 9-yard skeins)
DMC 319	Dark Forest Green (3)
DMC 3346	Dark Olive Green (2)
DMC 472	Light Olive Green (1)
DMC 743	Darkest Yellow (1)
DMC 745	Yellow (1)
Metallic Gold	Metallic Gold (16 yards)
DMC 746	Palest Yellow (1)
DMC 309	Red (1)
DMC 948	Palest Pink (1)
DMC 3325	Sky Blue (1)
DMC 806	Turquoise Green (1)
DMC 775	Palest Blue (1)
DMC 3687	Purple (1)
DMC 3706	Peach (1)

Color #	Color (# of 3-ply 33" strands)
EWP 1010	Cream (25)

MATERIALS

14 mesh Mono canvas (cut size: 13 x 11½ ")
Size 20 tapestry needle
13 shades DMC floss (use all 6 strands as it comes in the skein)
Metallic gold (use gold thread as it comes in the skein)
1 shade Persian yarn (use 1 strand of the 3-ply)

123 stitches x 103 stitches

The design as shown was worked on 14 mesh canvas, using Erica Wilson Persian yarn. To work on different sizes of mesh with other yarns refer to the conversion chart on p. 14.

Sèvres Porcelain Plaque (1773) from an Upright Secretary, 1775–80. Marie-Claude Sophie Xhrouet, French, active 1772–1788. GIFT OF SAMUEL H. KRESS FOUNDATION, 1958

Sèvres Fireboard

When Chinese porcelains first arrived in the West in the sixteenth century, they dazzled the world. Porcelain gets its name from the Venus shell, a shell so polished it has the sheen of china seen through glass. Discovering the secret of its manufacture took over one hundred years, because porcelain is made by firing together two natural materials at a very high temperature. The Chinese discovered this time consuming process which gives porcelain its unique and brilliant quality.

France's national porcelain factory is at Sèvres, just outside Paris. The first porcelain was made there in 1768, and although the styles of design changed, the manufacturing continued, even through the Revolution. Until 1793 each piece was stamped with the royal cipher and sets of the precious porcelain were specially made to be given to state visitors and public benefactors.

The Sèvres porcelain plaque, set into one of the two front panels of a gilded writing table or secretary, is the exquisite work of Marie-Claude-Sophie Xhrowet. She worked in the Sèvres factory from 1772 to 1788, following the footsteps of her father, who was active there from 1750 to 1775. Comparable pieces are in manor houses and museums all over the world, including the plaques set into a lacquer cabinet in the White Drawing Room of Windsor Castle in England.

Filled with roses, poppies, honeysuckle, morning glories, and tulips, this panel's basket is suspended from a lively bow of ribbon. Light and shade in subtle colors give the design its precious quality. In petit point, the design would make a beautiful *trumeau* (a panel set into the top of a mirror) or a square pillow with an oval center and a contrasting color for the surrounding "frame." Here, the ribbon has been condensed to make the design suitable for a fireboard. Worked on a large-scale canvas, it can give life to the dark fireplace in summertime.

MATERIALS

12 mesh Mono canvas (cut size: 26 x 25")
Size 18 tapestry needle
43 shades Persian yarn (separate and use only 2 strands of the 3-ply yarn)

240 stitches x 250 stitchess

The design as shown was worked on 12 mesh canvas, using Erica Wilson Persian yarn. To work on different sizes of mesh with other yarns refer to the chart on p. 126.

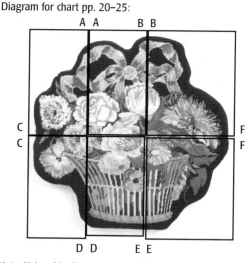

Diagram for chart pp. 20–25:

A A   B B

C   F
C   F

D D   E E

Note: Using this diagram as a guide, match up the letters and the dotted lines showing where the charts join. For instance, A is at the edge of your first chart, marked with a dotted line. On the second chart, A is five stitches in from the edge, also marked with a dotted line. **This is a five-stitch repeat which should not be worked**—it is there to help you establish your position when continuing on to the next chart.

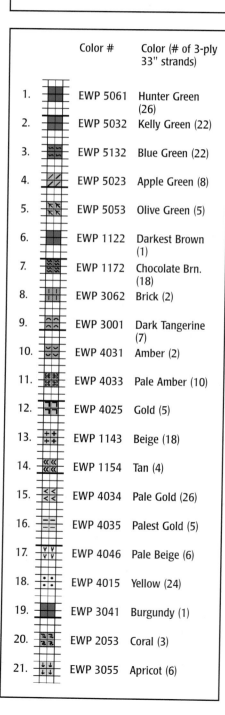

	Color #	Color (# of 3-ply 33" strands)
1.	EWP 5061	Hunter Green (26)
2.	EWP 5032	Kelly Green (22)
3.	EWP 5132	Blue Green (22)
4.	EWP 5023	Apple Green (8)
5.	EWP 5053	Olive Green (5)
6.	EWP 1122	Darkest Brown (1)
7.	EWP 1172	Chocolate Brn. (18)
8.	EWP 3062	Brick (2)
9.	EWP 3001	Dark Tangerine (7)
10.	EWP 4031	Amber (2)
11.	EWP 4033	Pale Amber (10)
12.	EWP 4025	Gold (5)
13.	EWP 1143	Beige (18)
14.	EWP 1154	Tan (4)
15.	EWP 4034	Pale Gold (26)
16.	EWP 4035	Palest Gold (5)
17.	EWP 4046	Pale Beige (6)
18.	EWP 4015	Yellow (24)
19.	EWP 3041	Burgundy (1)
20.	EWP 2053	Coral (3)
21.	EWP 3055	Apricot (6)

C

A · B

	Color #	Color (# of 3-ply 33" strands)
22.	EWP 3056	Pale Apricot (16)
23.	EWP 3005	Palest Apricot (10)
24.	EWP 2011	Wine (1)
25.	EWP 3041	Dark Red (12)
26.	EWP 2043	Dark Pink (2)
27.	EWP 2032	Dark Dusty Pink (4)
28.	EWP 2033	Dusty Pink (20)
29.	EWP 3066	Pale Peach (16)
30.	EWP 3034	Pale Dusty Pink (5)
31.	EWP 2035	Palest Dusty Pink (21)
32.	EWP 6013	Purple (17)
33.	EWP 6025	Rose Lavender (14)
34.	EWP 6026	Pale Rose Lav. (14)
35.	EWP 7002	Dark Blue (7)
36.	EWP 7004	Medium Blue (8)
37.	EWP 7006	Pale Blue (6)
38.	EWP 1073	Gray Blue (2)
39.	EWP 7024	Pale Blue Green (2)
40.	EWP 1074	Pale Gray Blue (6)
41.	EWP 5065	Mint (2)
42.	EWP 1012	Oatmeal (16)
43.	EWP 1050	Black (80)

Note: For clarity, the background color black has not been added to the chart. If you prefer, you may use another color for the background. You may change the shape of the border, or you may follow the outline as indicated on the diagram or as shown in the photograph.

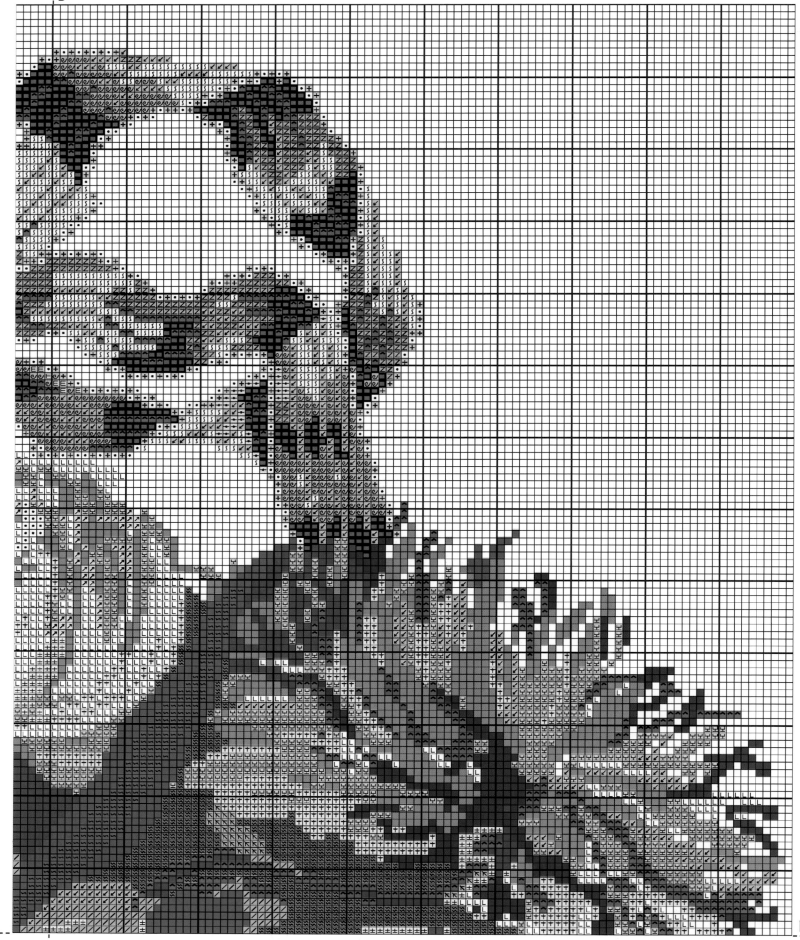

B

F

(joins p. 25)

(joins p. 20)

C

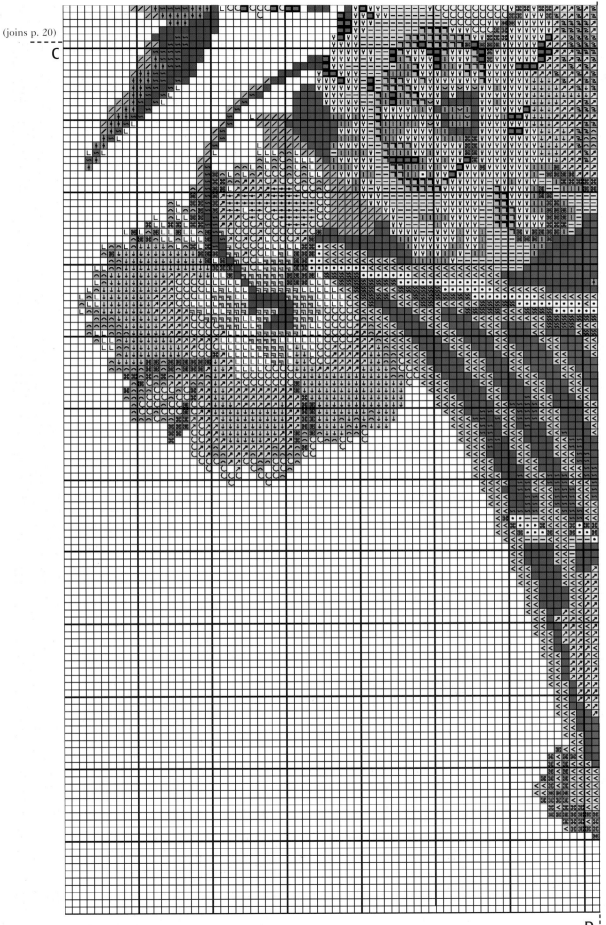

D

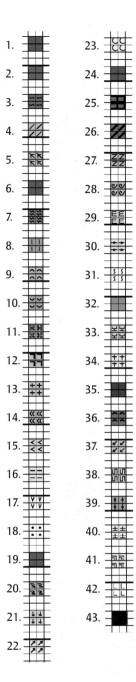

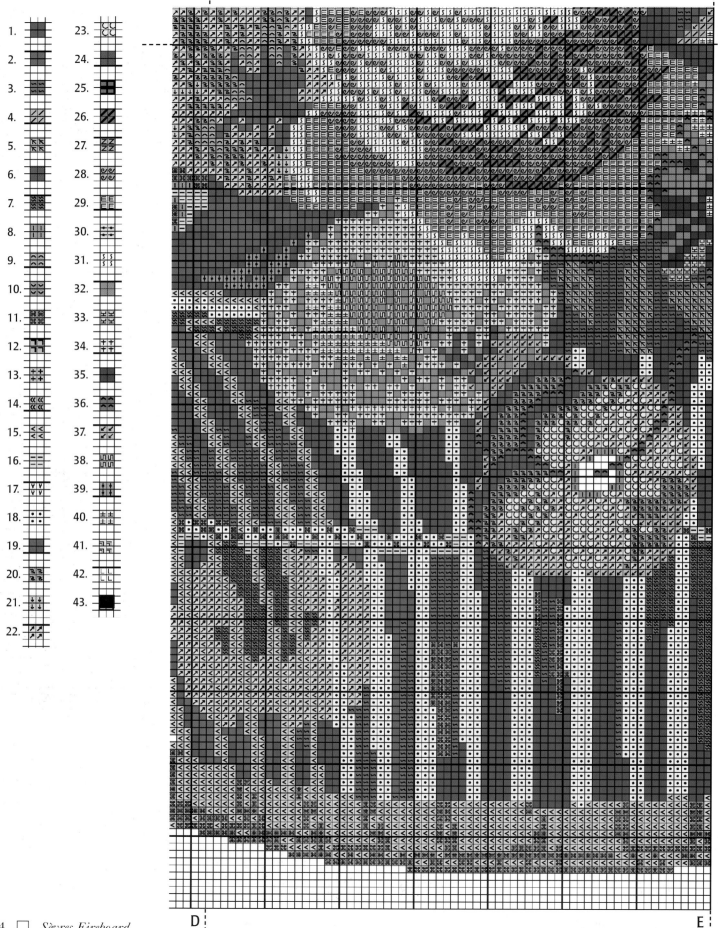

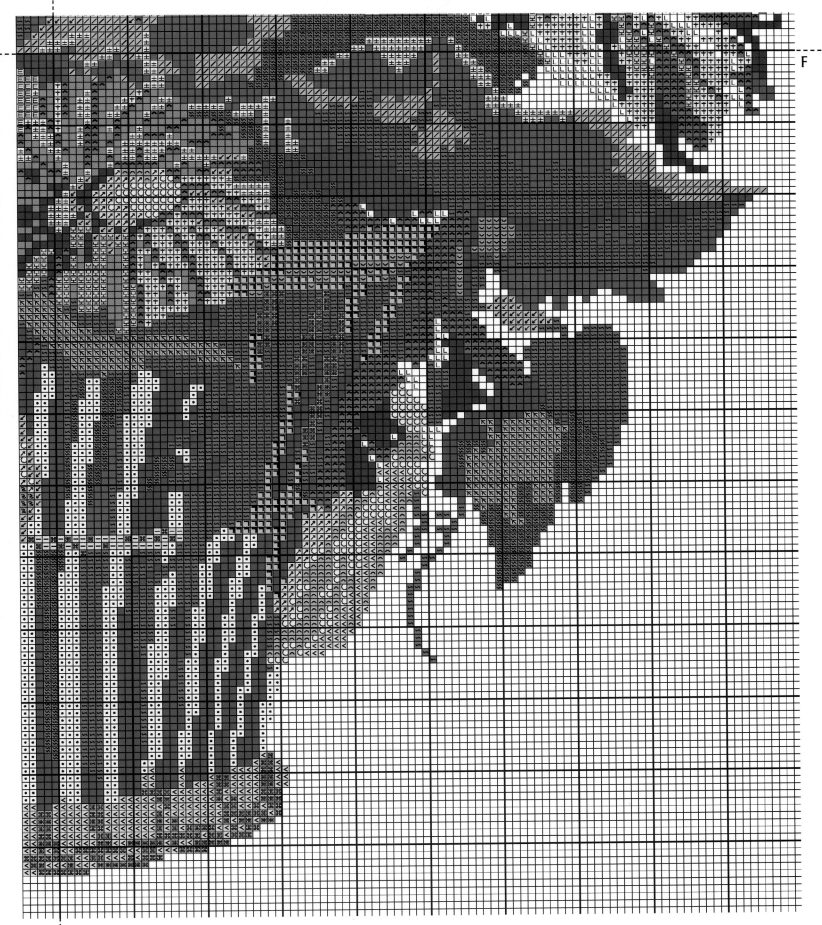

F

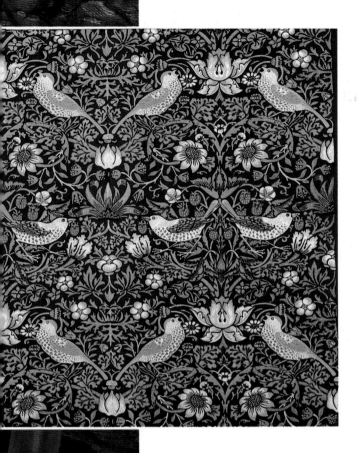

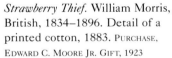

Strawberry Thief. William Morris, British, 1834–1896. Detail of a printed cotton, 1883. PURCHASE, EDWARD C. MOORE JR. GIFT, 1923

William Morris

Artist, craftsman, and poet William Morris (1834–1896) established his first factory in England in 1861, producing furniture, hand-blocked linens, wallpapers, and embroideries. Morris felt that art should be appreciated by all and should be a part of everyone's life. In 1890 he founded a printing press. His work influenced architecture and interior design as well as printing and typography. It was at his workshop in Merton Abbey that he made his first printing of the pattern he called the "Strawberry Thief" shown here.

William Morris's textile and wallpaper designs were inspired by Asian influences and maintained a two-dimensional effect. This, he believed, was more in keeping with the flat surface of the wall, rather than three-dimensional illusion.

Because the shapes are stylized with little or no shading in a repeat pattern, William Morris's designs are easily adaptable to any size. By adding more repeats and by working on a larger mesh, the child's chairseat shown here, for example, could become an area rug or a bench. Also, the Compton flower, shown here in pink and green with a blue ground, may also be effective in blue and white. Experimenting in differences of scale and color with these designs can bring satisfactory results.

MATERIALS

14 mesh Mono canvas (cut size: 20 x 13½")
Size 20 tapestry needle
12 shades Persian yarn (separate and use only 1 strand of the 3-ply yarn)

225 stitches x 191 stitches

The design as shown was worked on 14 mesh canvas, using Erica Wilson Persian yarn. To work on different sizes of mesh with other yarns refer to the chart on p. 126.

Diagram for chart pp. 28–33:

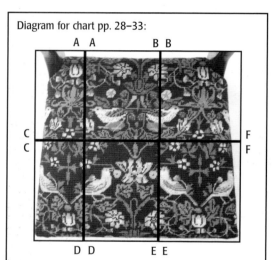

A A   B B

C   F
C   F

D D   E E

<u>Note</u>: Using this diagram as a guide, match up the letters and the dotted lines showing where the charts join. For instance, <u>A</u> is at the edge of your first chart, marked with a dotted line. On the second chart, <u>A</u> is five stitches in from the edge, also marked with a dotted line. **This is a five-stitch repeat which should not be worked**—it is there to help you establish your position when continuing on to the next chart.

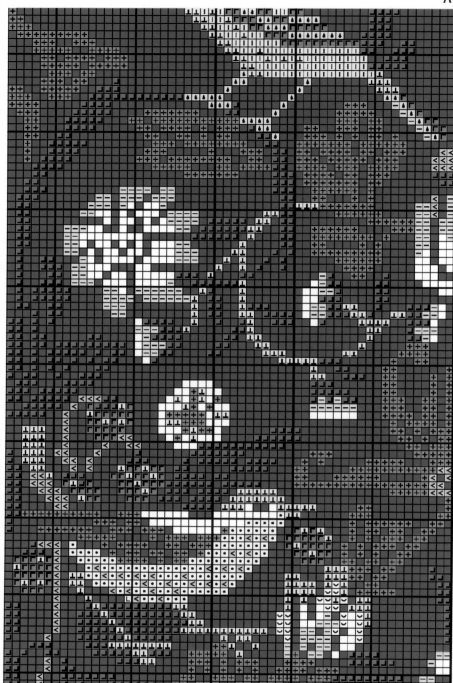

A

C

	Color #	Color (# of 3-ply 33" strands)
1.	EWP 7011	Navy Blue (75)
2.	EWP 7004	Sky Blue (28)
3.	EWP 5013	Pea Green (28)
4.	EWP 2051	Red (12)

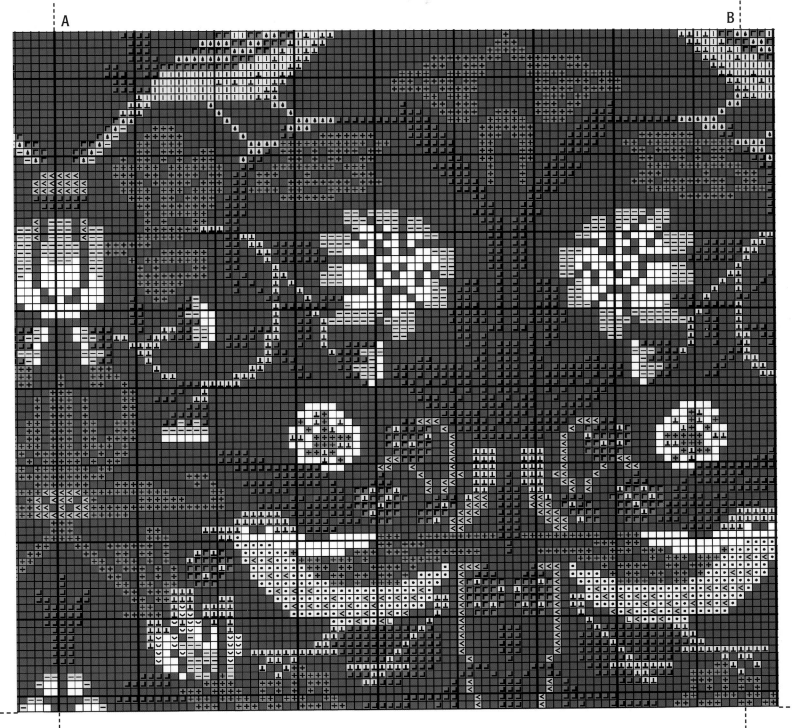

	Color #	Color (# of 3-ply 33" strands)
5.	EWP 2035	Pale Pink (6)
6.	EWP 2046	Pink (14)
7.	EWP 3055	Tangerine (6)
8.	EWP 4012	Yellow (12)

	Color #	Color (# of 3-ply 33" strands)
9.	EWP 1012	Cream (3)
10.	EWP 3036	Pale Peach (8)
11.	EWP 4015	Pale Yellow (2)
12.	EWP 1001	White (10)

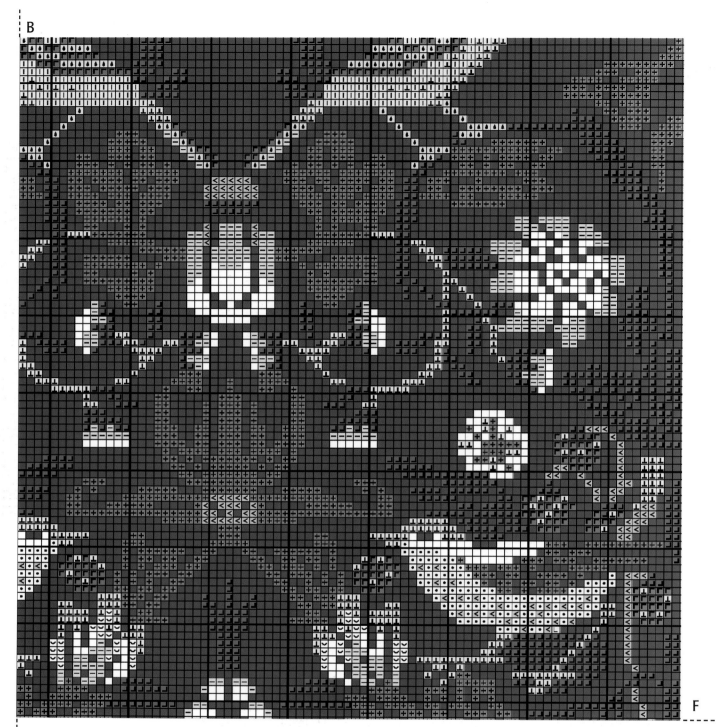

F

(joins p. 33)

(joins p. 28)

C

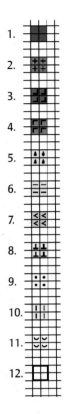

1.
2.
3.
4.
5.
6.
7.
8.
9.
10.
11.
12.

D

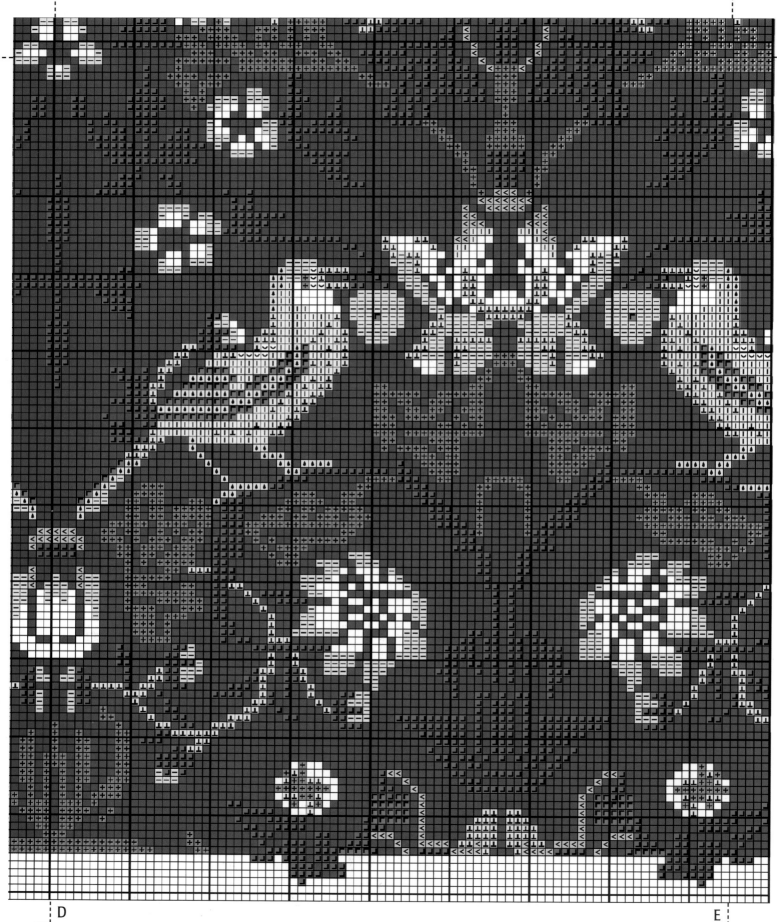

D

E

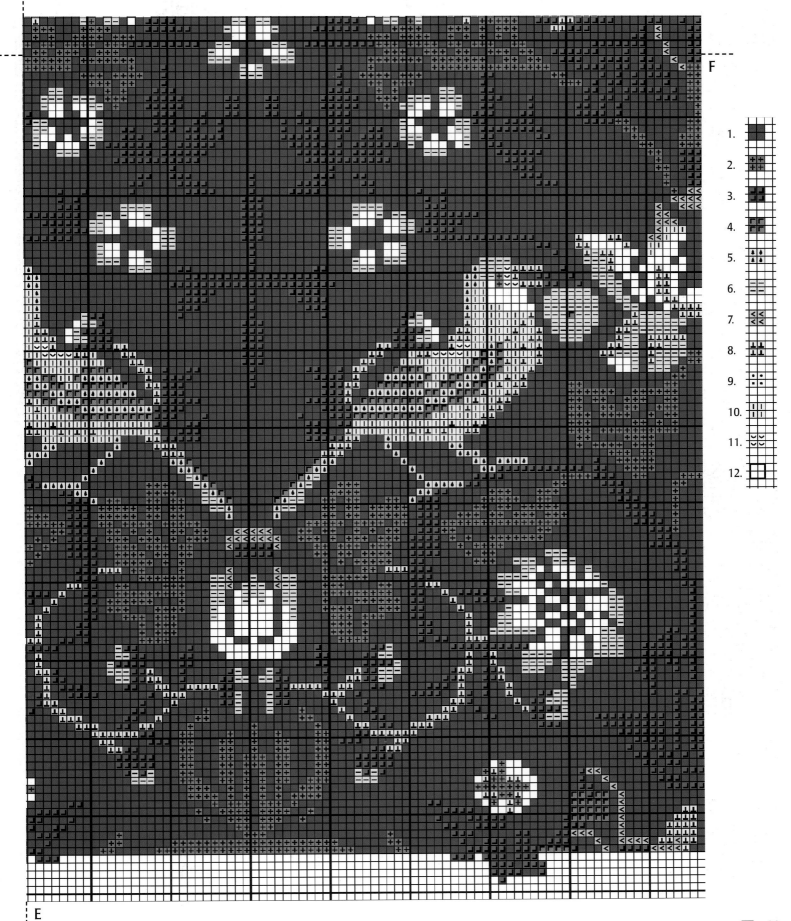

F

E

Textile Design. French, second quarter
of the 19th century. Gouache on cardboard.

French Textile Design

The French textile design that inspired our oval rug is
one of a series of patterns painted on thin cardboard in
gouache during the second quarter of the nineteenth century. The designs are characterized by their brilliant colors,
dramatic highlights, and strong shadows, set against dark
backgrounds. Unlike the Berlin patterns, which were
often painted on grids so that they could be counted onto
needlepoint canvas, these designs are on plain backgrounds. Several have fringes painted on one side, which
might suggest that they were designed for woven rugs or
shawls. Bold shadings and strong color contrasts enable
the designs to be worked on a large mesh canvas without
losing the clean lines. The subtle blending of colors
makes this needlepoint fascinating to work.

Because they were designed expressly for textiles, like
the Berlin patterns of a later date (see p. 53), each color is
clearly distinguishable, even though the final result appears
to be a blending of shades. Since the borders around the
rug are separate and self-contained, any section could be
worked out on finer mesh as a mirror in a frame, eyeglass
case, handbag, or even a belt.

MATERIALS

12 mesh Mono canvas (cut size: 36 x 27")
Size 18 tapestry needle
39 shades Persian yarn (separate and use only 2 strands of the 3-ply yarn)

370 stitches x 260 stitches

The design as shown was worked on 12 mesh canvas, using Erica Wilson Persian yarn. To work on different sizes of mesh with other yarns refer to the chart on p. 126.

		Color #	Color (# of 3-ply 33" strands)
1.		EWP 1012	Cream (60)
2.		EWP 4016	Palest Yellow (9)
3.		EWP 4015	Pale Yellow (5)
4.		EWP 4028	Pale Gold (9)
5.		EWP 4046	Stone (1)
6.		EWP 4026	Gold (3)
7.		EWP 4034	Pale Amber (8)
8.		EWP 3056	Pale Apricot (20)
9.		EWP 4043	Khaki (14)
10.		EWP 1144	Tan (5)
11.		EWP 1154	Dark Stone (4)
12.		EWP 3091	Amber (6)
13.		EWP 5092	Fir Green (50)
14.		EWP 1124	Chocolate (9)
15.		EWP 3066	Pale Peach (7)
16.		EWP 3055	Apricot (3)
17.		EWP 3044	Salmon (14)
18.		EWP 3001	Burnt Orange (8)
19.		EWP 2053	Rose (8)
20.		EWP 2031	Brick (60)

Diagram for chart pp. 36–45:

Note: Using this diagram as a guide, match up the letters and the dotted lines showing where the charts join. For instance, A is at the edge of your first chart, marked with a dotted line. On the second chart, A is five stitches in from the edge, also marked with a dotted line. **This is a five-stitch repeat which should not be worked**—it is there to help you establish your position when continuing on to the next chart.

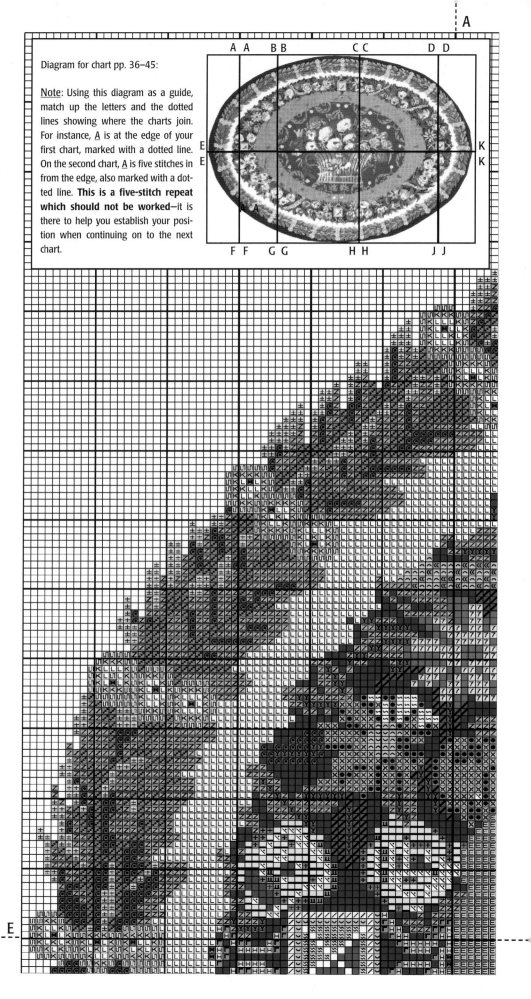

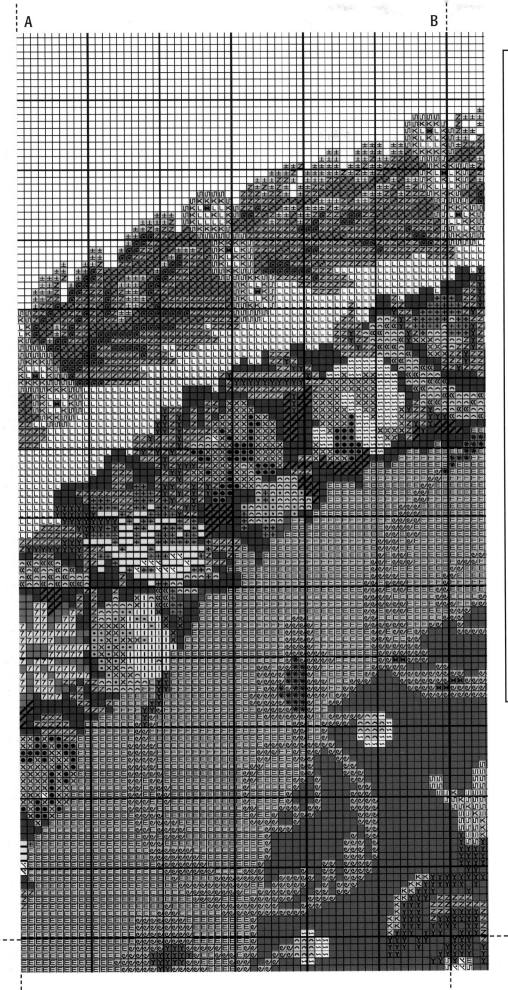

		Color #	Color (# of 3-ply 33" strands)
21.		EWP 2049	Pale Pink (20)
22.		EWP 2035	Pale Dusty Rose (5)
23.		EWP 2034	Dusty Rose (18)
24.		EWP 6027	Rose Lavender (19)
25.		EWP 6005	Lavender (22)
26.		EWP 2013	Mauve (12)
27.		EWP 2032	Pale Brick (14)
28.		EWP 7095	Aqua (8)
29.		EWP 7046	Blue (75)
30.		EWP 7033	Spruce (2)
31.		EWP 5133	Celadon Green (6)
32.		EWP 7022	Blue Green (20)
33.		EWP 5061	Hunter Green (45)
34.		EWP 5045	Pale Olive (45)
35.		EWP 5004	Sage (60)
36.		EWP 5132	Medium Green (38)
37.		EWP 5063	Apple Green (10)
38.		EWP 5013	Bright Pea (23)
39.		EWP 5005	Pale Sage (28)
40.		EWP 1001	White (5)

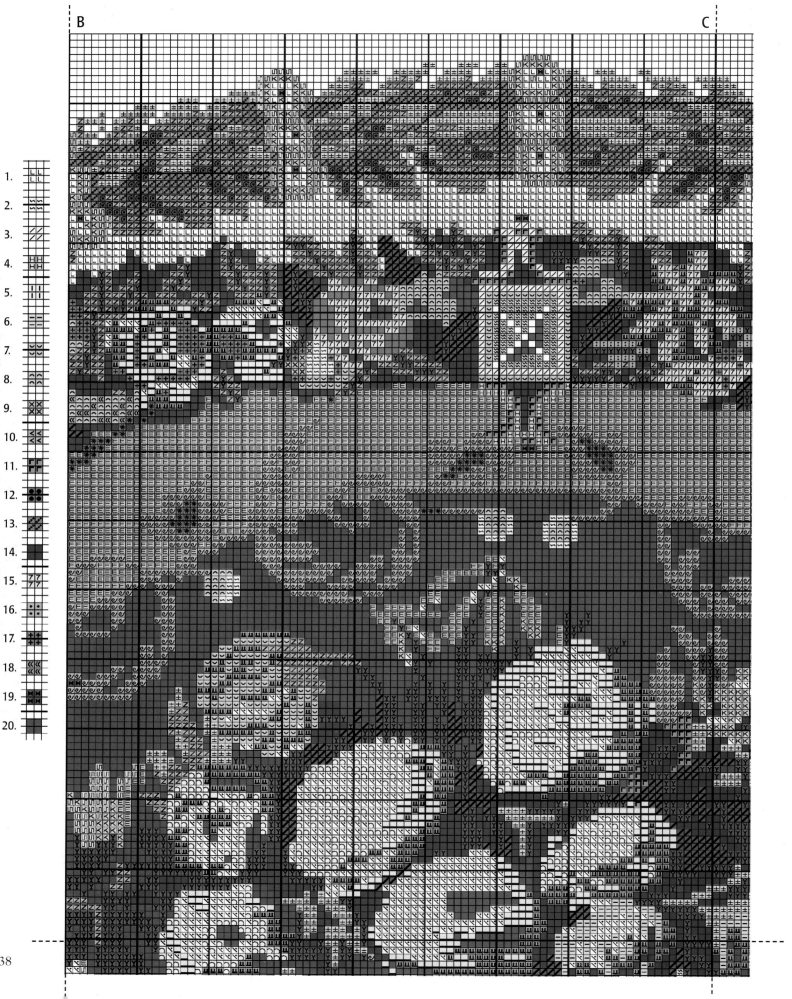

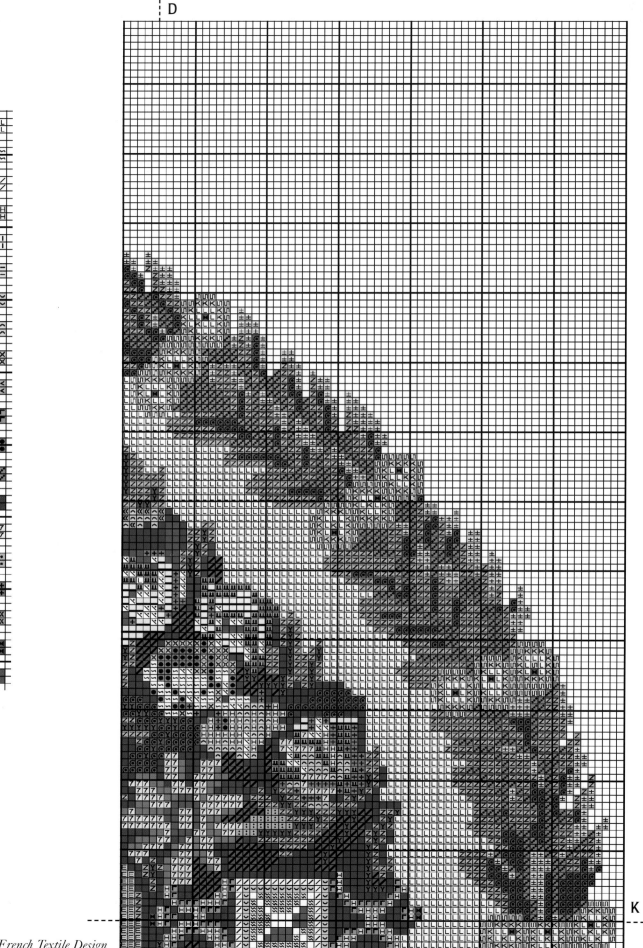

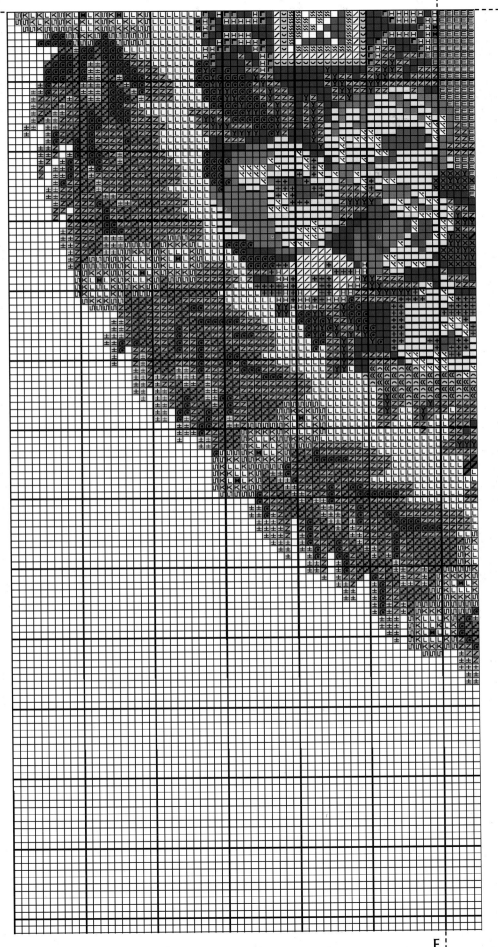

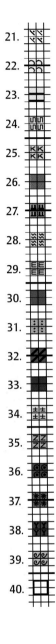

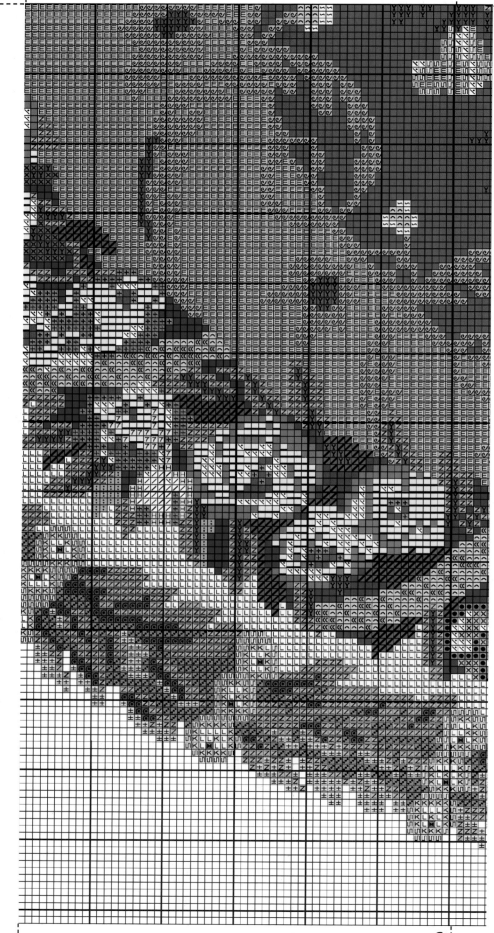

1.
2.
3.
4.
5.
6.
7.
8.
9.
10.
11.
12.
13.
14.
15.
16.
17.
18.
19.
20.

G

G

H

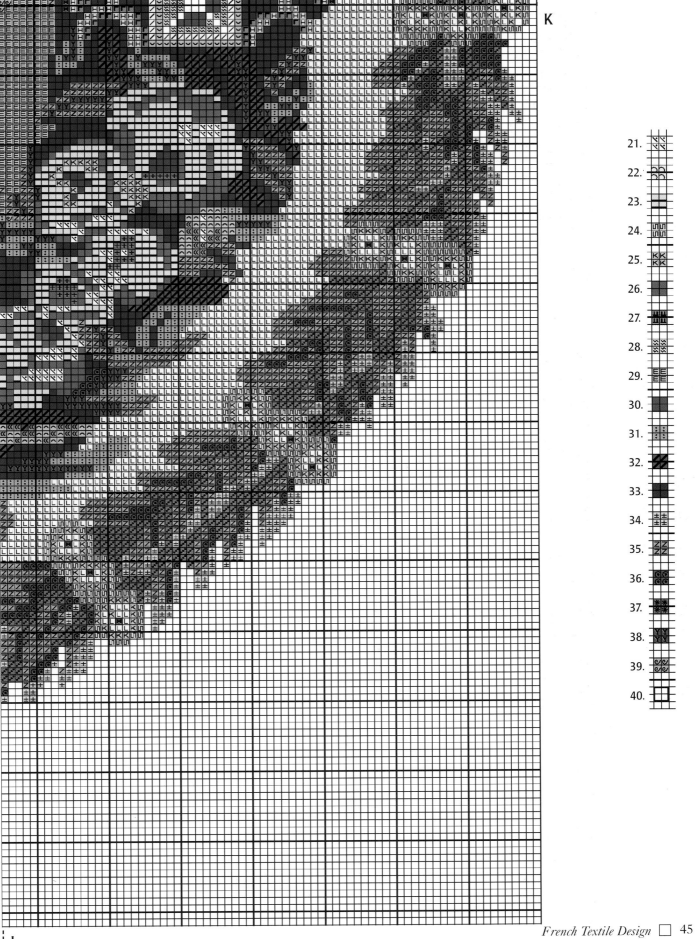

K

21.
22.
23.
24.
25.
26.
27.
28.
29.
30.
31.
32.
33.
34.
35.
36.
37.
38.
39.
40.

J

Grapevine. Leaded-glass window.
Tiffany Studios, New York City, c. 1905.
GIFT OF RUTH AND FRANK STANTON, 1978

Tiffany Window—Grapevine

Louis Comfort Tiffany, America's Art Nouveau master, gained international renown for his superior design techniques. Tiffany experimented with ways to produce iridescent colors using his own completely new technique called Favrile. Beginning in 1892, the Tiffany Studios produced a variety of handcrafted objects such as stained-glass windows, panels, fire screens, suites of furniture, enameled boxes, jewelry, tableware, clocks, desk sets, as well as interiors for private residences. Tiffany's own artistic priority was his windows, but he later began to manufacture his popular lamps to utilize off-cuts of glass too small to incorporate into the larger designs.

Several of Tiffany's most important stained-glass pieces are displayed in a spacious setting in the Museum's American Wing. One of these is a large window with a trellis entwined with grapes, from which our detail for the needlepoint is taken. Every angle from which the window is viewed changes the colors of the glass and the iridescence of each shade, so that interpreting this with wools is a delightful challenge. The dramatic effect is heightened by the contrast of the blue-purple grapes and the peacock green leaves on a subtle background of soft greens and golds.

Since the design is so intricate it is best framed as a panel or hung as a tapestry with its own needlepoint border forming the frame. It is difficult to select just one design from the Tiffany stained-glass masterpieces. The technique of stained glass separates each color, making the design particularly well suited to needlepoint. Once you have worked the grapes and experimented with the blending of colors, you may be inspired to try another design.

A

B

Diagram for chart pp. 48–51:

Note: Using this diagram as a guide, match up the letters and the dotted lines showing where the charts join. For instance, A is at the edge of your first chart, marked with a dotted line. On the second chart, A is five stitches in from the edge, also marked with a dotted line. This is a five-stitch repeat which should not be worked—it is there to help you establish your position when continuing on to the next chart.

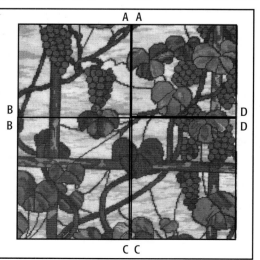

A A

B

B

D

D

C C

48 □ *Tiffany Window—Grapevine*

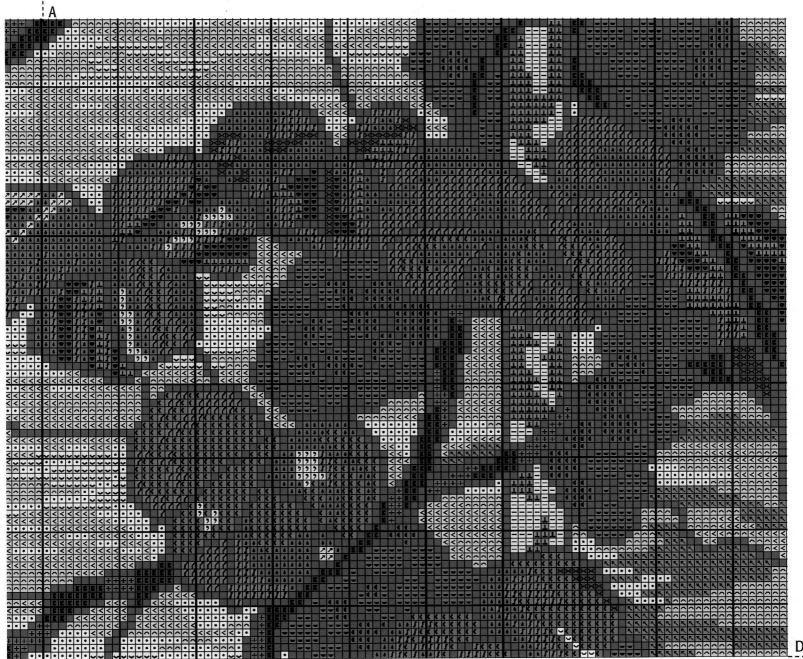

A

D

	Color #	Color (# of 3-ply 33" strands)
1.	EWP 7131	Deep Sea Blue (60)
2.	EWP 7132	Navy Blue (12)
3.	EWP 7121	Royal Blue (10)
4.	EWP 7111	Brilliant Blue (12)
5.	EWP 7112	Medium Blue (14)
6.	EWP 7124	Pale Blue (6)
7.	EWP 1017	Palest Blue (3)
8.	EWP 7093	Turquoise (6)
9.	EWP 7094	Pale Turquoise (9)
10.	EWP 7096	Palest Turquoise (55)
11.	EWP 5061	Hunter Green (9)
12.	EWP 5011	Olive Green (20)
13.	EWP 5081	Dark Kelly Green (26)
14.	EWP 5082	Kelly Green (18)
15.	EWP 5022	Apple Green (4)
16.	EWP 5023	Pale Apple (2)
17.	EWP 5033	Bright Grass Green (55)
18.	EWP 5036	Pale Grass Green (40)
19.	EWP 6032	Violet (9)
20.	EWP 6022	Plum (15)
21.	EWP 3066	Peach (2)
22.	EWP 4015	Maize (55)

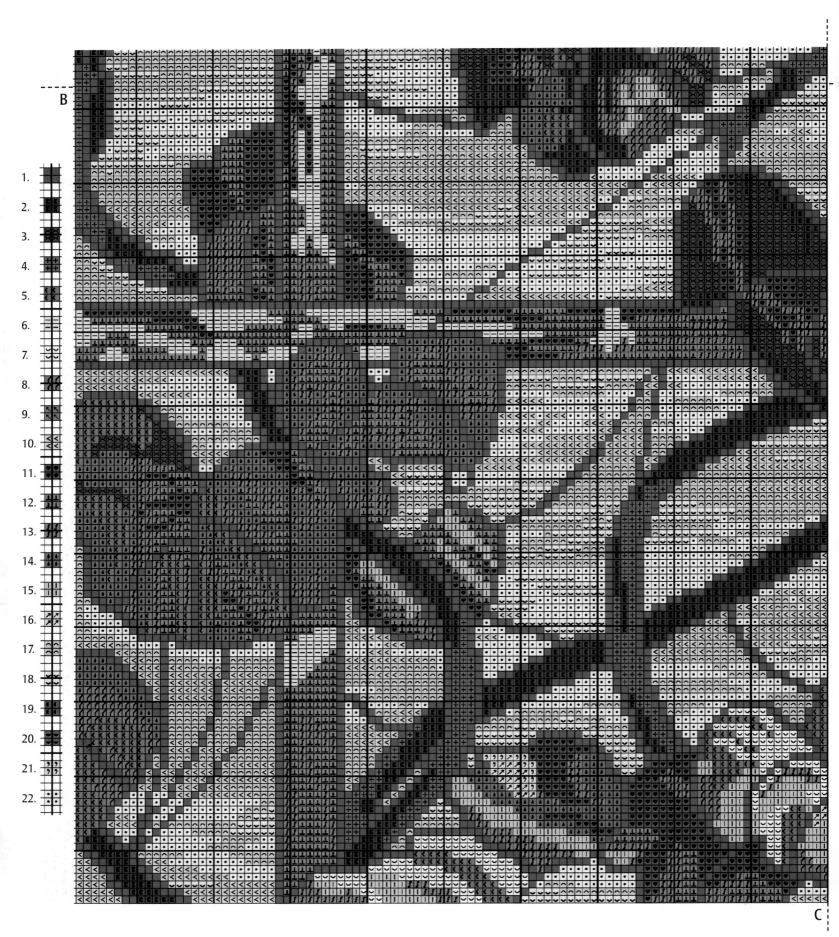

Quinces

In 1810, a Berlin printseller named L. W. Wittich, whose wife was a needlewoman, produced the first patterns drawn on "point paper"—a basic grid ruled on paper with each square colored in. This was then copied onto canvas by counting, stitch by stitch. Because the squaring enabled the artist to get perfect repeats, geometric designs could be combined with realistic ones, and soon Berlin wool work became so popular that all work on canvas was known by that name.

Many geometric patterns were counted and collected on strips of canvas so that different color schemes could be worked out. Just one or two repeats were stitched on these "samplers," so they could be copied onto any of the many needlepoint projects. The colors were deep, rich jewel shades, many of the patterns being particularly suitable for beadwork. Some designs were in silk but most fashionable were those in cross-stitch in wool on canvas.

The Quinces pattern is based on one of the designs from a strip sampler of Berlin wool work. It may be worked in the universal tent stitch used now for needlepoint, or in cross-stitch like the original Berlin work, making each square just like the graph.

The character of each pattern can be completely transformed when the colors are altered. For instance, substituting a light background for a dark one can change the pattern's entire effect as shown here. The half worked sample at left shows how the outlines of the shapes are counted out first. Then the colors can be filled in with little or no counting.

Quinces. English, late 19th century. Wool and silk embroidered on canvas.
ANONYMOUS GIFT, 1987

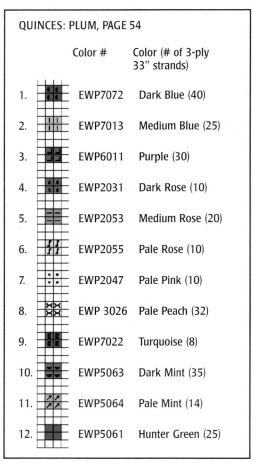

	Color #	Color (# of 3-ply 33" strands)
1.	EWP7072	Dark Blue (40)
2.	EWP7013	Medium Blue (25)
3.	EWP6011	Purple (30)
4.	EWP2031	Dark Rose (10)
5.	EWP2053	Medium Rose (20)
6.	EWP2055	Pale Rose (10)
7.	EWP2047	Pale Pink (10)
8.	EWP 3026	Pale Peach (32)
9.	EWP7022	Turquoise (8)
10.	EWP5063	Dark Mint (35)
11.	EWP5064	Pale Mint (14)
12.	EWP5061	Hunter Green (25)

	Color #	Color
1.	EWP 5131	Hunter (8)
2.	EWP 5132	Blue Grass (22)
3.	EWP 5006	Lt. Celadon Green (20)
4.	EWP 5005	Celadon Green (8)
5.	EWP 2053	Red (10)
6.	EWP 3045	Orange (10)
7.	EWP 3046	Apricot (16)
8.	EWP 4056	Pale Gold (20)
9.	EWP 4054	Gold (8)
10.	EWP 1145	Khaki (40)
11.	EWP 7004	Heron Blue (10)
12.	EWP 7006	Sky Blue (10)
13.	EWP 1001	Snow White (40)

MATERIALS

14 mesh Mono canvas (cut size: 18 x 18")
Size 20 tapestry needle
13 (12) shades Persian yarn (separate and use only
    1 strand of the 3-ply yarn)

201 stitches x 210 stitches

The design as shown was worked on 14 mesh canvas, using Erica Wilson Persian yarn. To work on different sizes of mesh with other yarns refer to the chart on p.126.

Diagram for chart pp. 54–55:

Note: The Quinces design is a repeat pattern of stars and quinces. These two charts represent a section of the pillow (one worked in Plum, p. 54, and the other in Apricot, p. 55). They show the alternating colors for placement only. Begin by stitching the outlines of the stars and quinces in one color, as shown on page 53, starting at the center of the canvas. Once your outline is completed, you can easily fill in the remaining colors. The finished pillow has 5 complete stars across and down, and 4 complete and 2 half quinces across and down.

Blue-and-White Porcelain

The rare and beautiful blue-and-white porcelains of China and Japan were curiosities in sixteenth-century Europe. Quick to realize the potential market, the Dutch and British East India Companies began importing the beautiful vases, pots, and bowls, and by the seventeenth century, "China-mania" as it was called, was in full swing on a grand scale. Every fashionable country house, castle, or palace in Holland, France, Germany, or England had walls lined with arrangements of porcelain. The extent of the numbers involved is evidenced by the recent salvage of a Chinese Junk bound for Indonesia and sunk in 1690. On board were more than twenty-eight thousand jugs, jars, goblets, and vases, all in blue and white!

When the Asian secrets of making porcelain finally found their way to Europe, collecting blue and white became even more widespread. By the late eighteenth century, "Chinese Export" china as it was called, was an important part of many a colonial household's decor. Indeed it continued well into the nineteenth century on both sides of the Atlantic as is evidenced by the famous Peacock Room built by Frederick R. Leyland, the British shipping magnate.

Leyland added the large dining room to his London house expressly to show off his extensive collections of blue-and-white china. Since Leyland's friend, the American artist James McNeill Whistler, was also a collector of blue and white, it was fitting that his painting *Rose and Silver: The Princess from the Land of Porcelain* should be hanging in the center of the room. Charles Lang Freer, Whistler's patron, acquired the room and in 1920 reassembled it at the Freer Gallery in Washington, D.C. Now that blue and white is fashionable again, the room has been restored to its original splendor with porcelain from private collections.

Today, we can decorate our homes with pillows in the shapes of vases, with chords and tassels looped around their necks as pictured opposite.

Above: Porcelain Plate. Chinese, late Ming dynasty, late 16th–early 17th century. ROGERS FUND, 1916

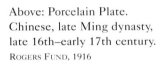

Below: Porcelain Jar. Chinese, Ming dynasty, 15th century. GIFT OF ROBERT E. TOD, 1937. PHOTOGRAPH BY SCHECTER LEE

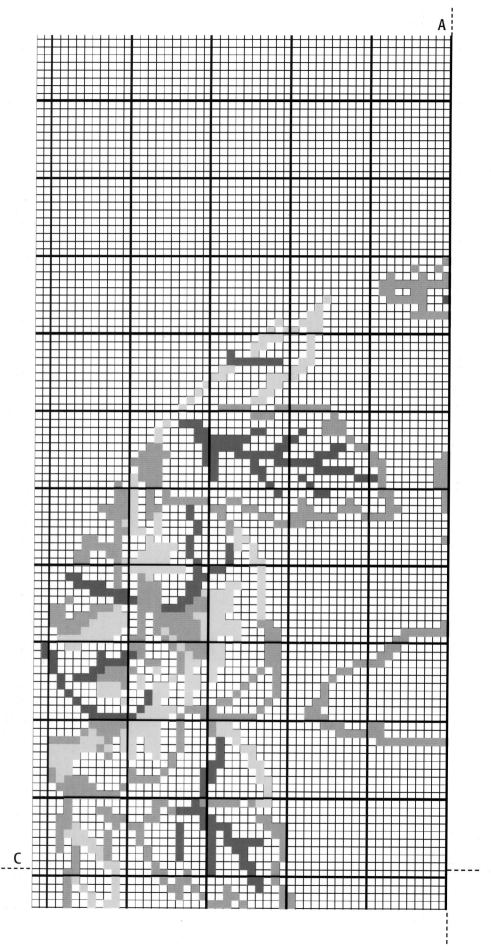

MATERIALS

14 mesh Mono canvas (cut size: 19 x 18")
Size 20 tapestry needle
4 shades Persian yarn (separate and use
only 1 strand of the 3-ply yarn)

199 stitches x 235 stitches

The design as shown was worked on 14 mesh
canvas, using Erica Wilson Persian yarn. To work
on different sizes of mesh with other yarns refer
to the chart on p. 126.

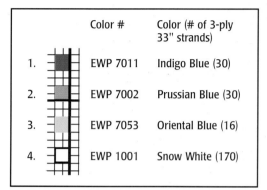

		Color #	Color (# of 3-ply 33" strands)
1.		EWP 7011	Indigo Blue (30)
2.		EWP 7002	Prussian Blue (30)
3.		EWP 7053	Oriental Blue (16)
4.		EWP 1001	Snow White (170)

Diagram for chart pp. 58–63:

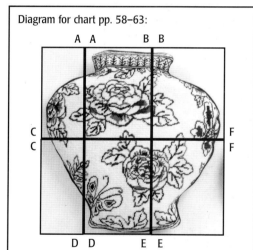

Note: Using this diagram as a guide, match up the letters and the dotted lines showing where the charts join. For instance, <u>A</u> is at the edge of your first chart, marked with a dotted line. On the second chart, <u>A</u> is five stitches in from the edge, also marked with a dotted line. **This is a five-stitch repeat which should not be worked**—it is there to help you establish your position when continuing on to the next chart.

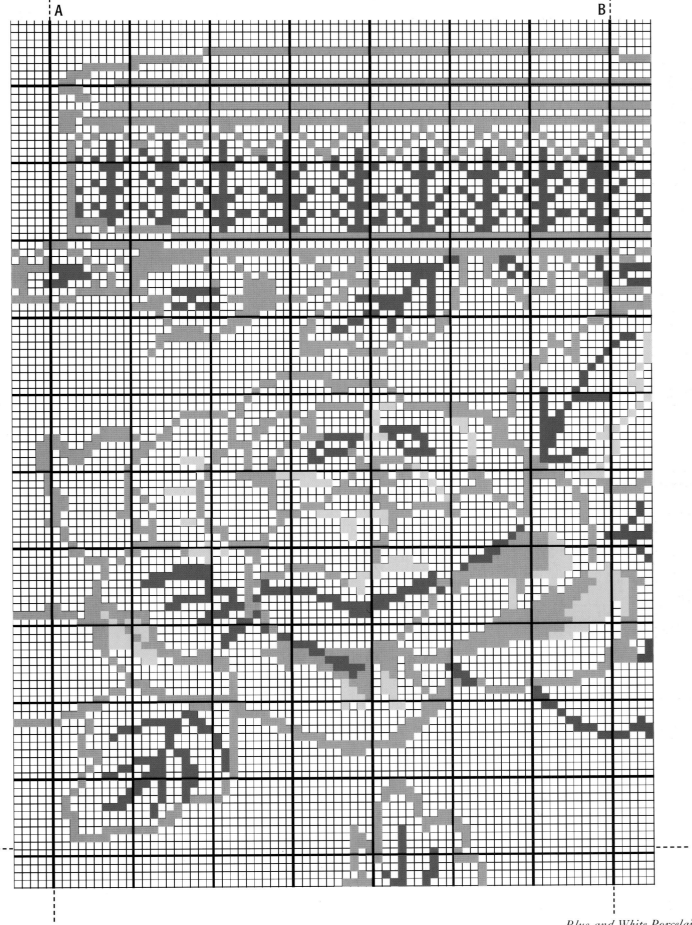

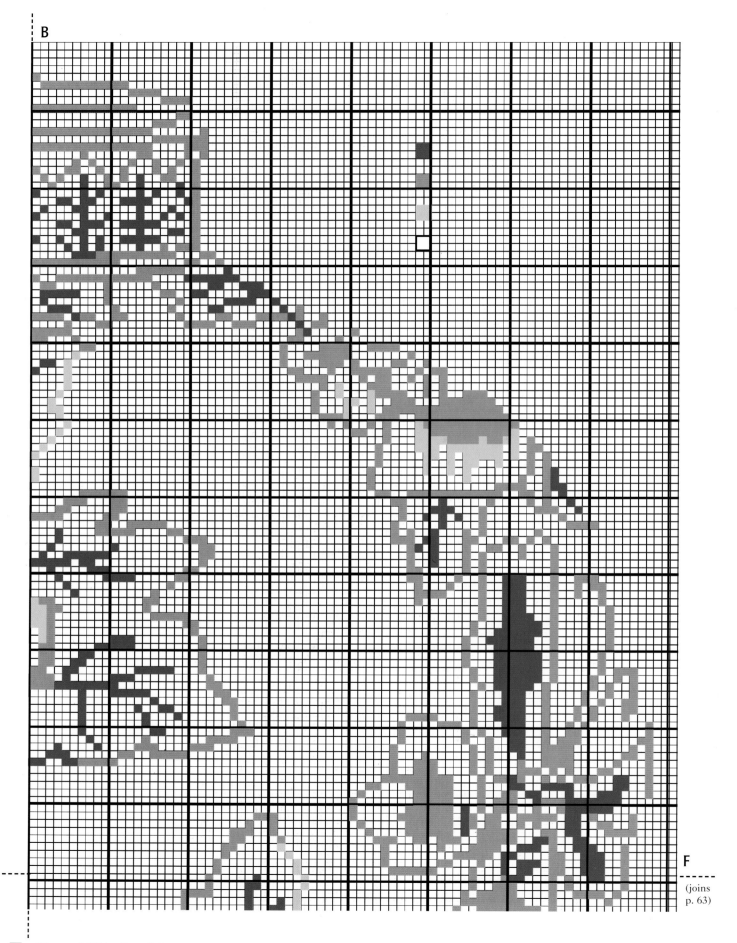

F

(joins p. 63)

(joins
p. 58)

C

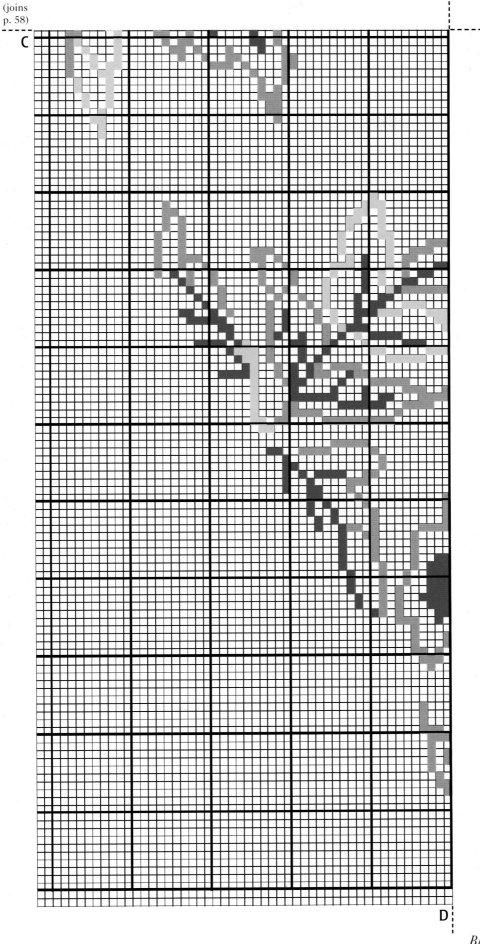

1.
2.
3.
4.

D

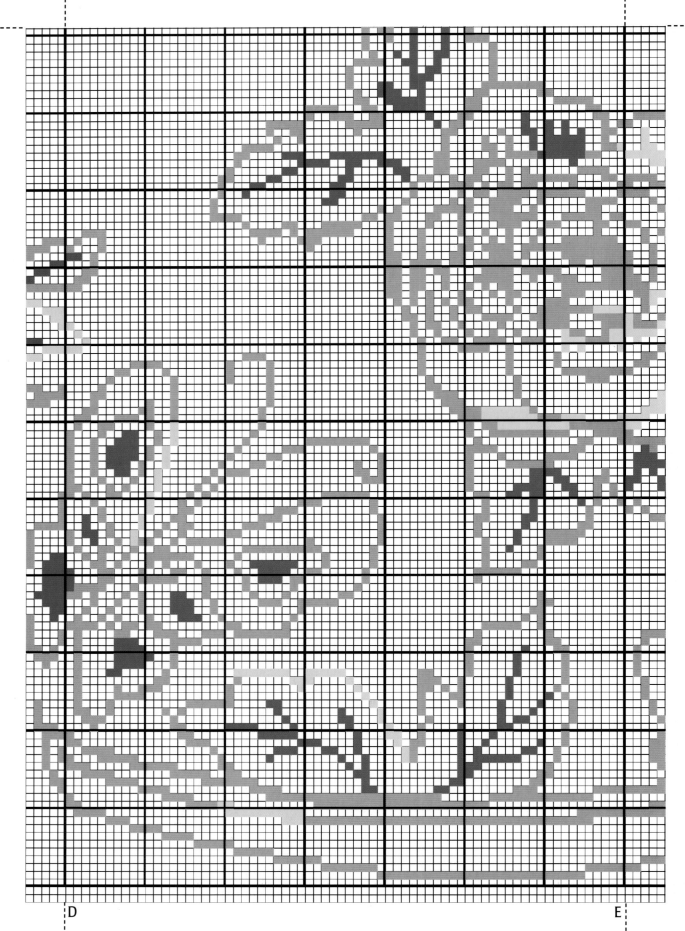

D

E

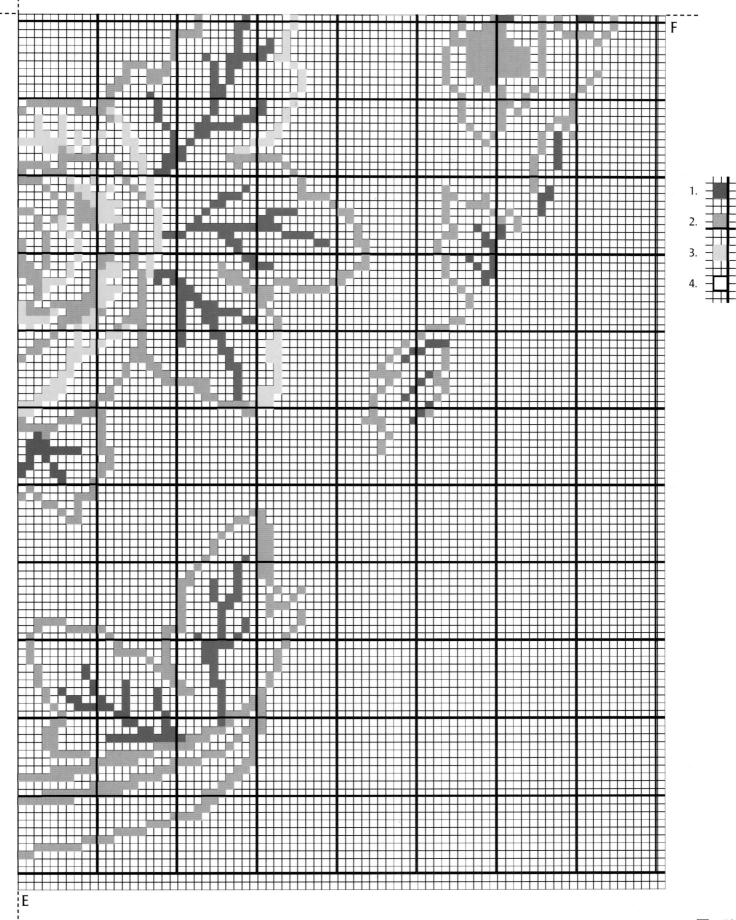

F

E

MATERIALS

14 mesh Mono canvas (cut size 18½ x 14½")
Size 20 tapestry needle
5 shades Persian yarn (separate and use only 1 strand of the 3-ply yarn)

263 stitches x 143 stitches

The design as shown was worked on 14 mesh canvas, using Erica Wilson Persian yarn. To work on different sizes of mesh with other yarns refer to the chart on p. 126.

	Color #	Color (# of 3-ply 33" strands)
1.	EWP7011	Indigo Blue (65)
2.	EWP7111	Ultramarine Blue (10)
3.	EWP7112	Oriental Blue (6)
4.	EWP7086	Pale Oriental Blue (17)
5.	EWP1001	Snow White (140)

Diagram for chart pp. 64–69:

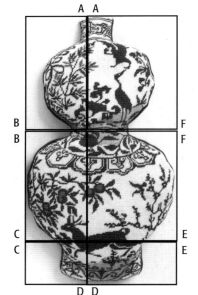

Note: Using this diagram as a guide, match up the letters and the dotted lines showing where the charts join. For instance, <u>A</u> is at the edge of your first chart, marked with a dotted line. On the second chart, <u>A</u> is five stitches in from the edge, also marked with a dotted line. **This is a five-stitch repeat which should not be worked**—it is there to help you establish your position when continuing on to the next chart.

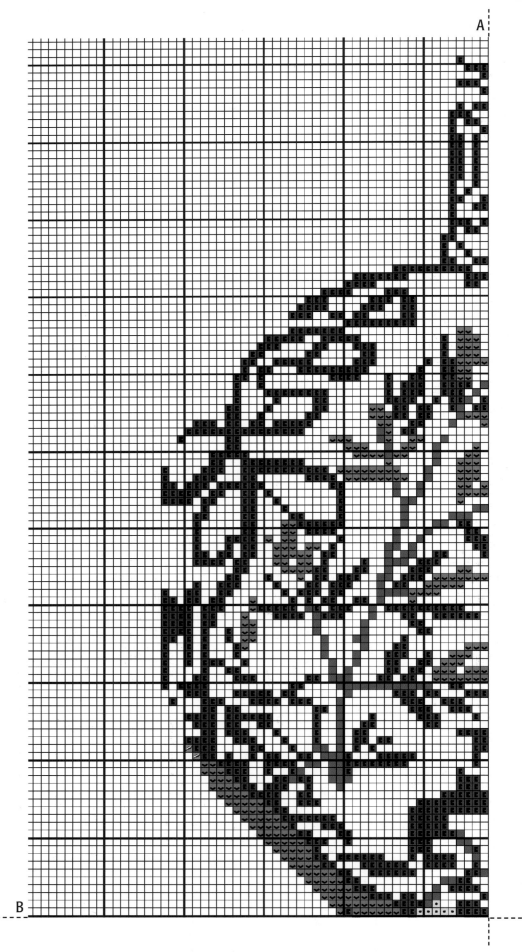

A

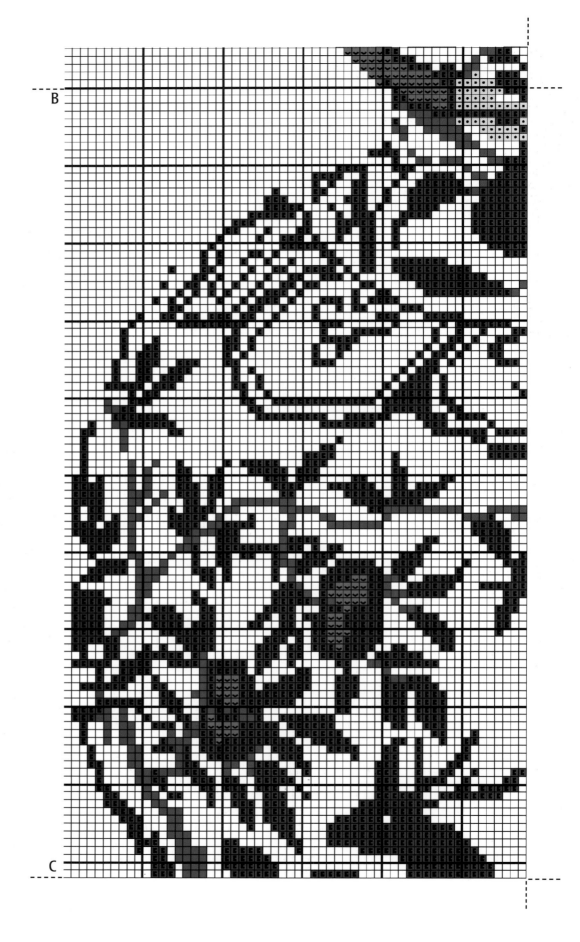

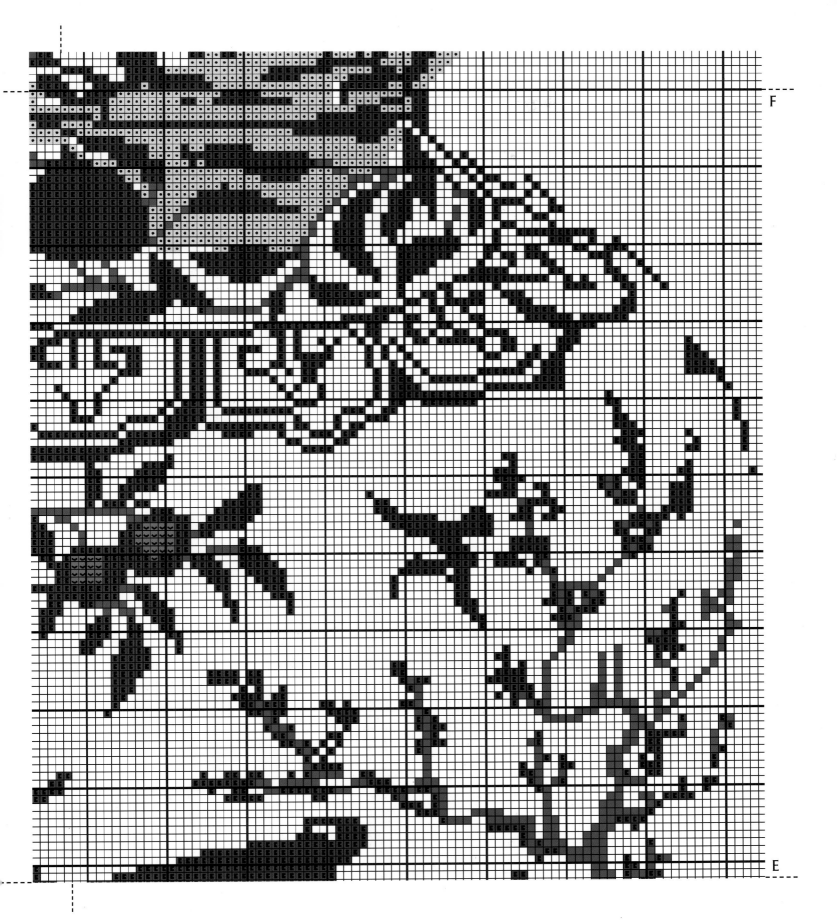

D

E

Table Carpet with Unicorns. Dutch, mid-17th century.
Wool and silk. GIFT OF P. A.B. WIDENER, 1970

Oriental rugs were so prized in seventeenth-century Europe that they were used to dress tables rather than floors. European weavers also made their own adaptations of Asian carpets, and Dutch examples such as this one typically have central medallions surrounded by lush fruit and foliate decoration. The border, which repeats the central motif on a smaller scale, would have fallen over the table's sides. Since the unicorn is a symbol of virginity, the carpet may have originally been made for an unmarried girl.

When adapting the table carpet to needlepoint, the unicorn can be best stitched on fourteen or eighteen mesh canvas in order to reproduce each fine detail. The pillow can also be adorned with piping in velvet or boxed with cords and tassels.

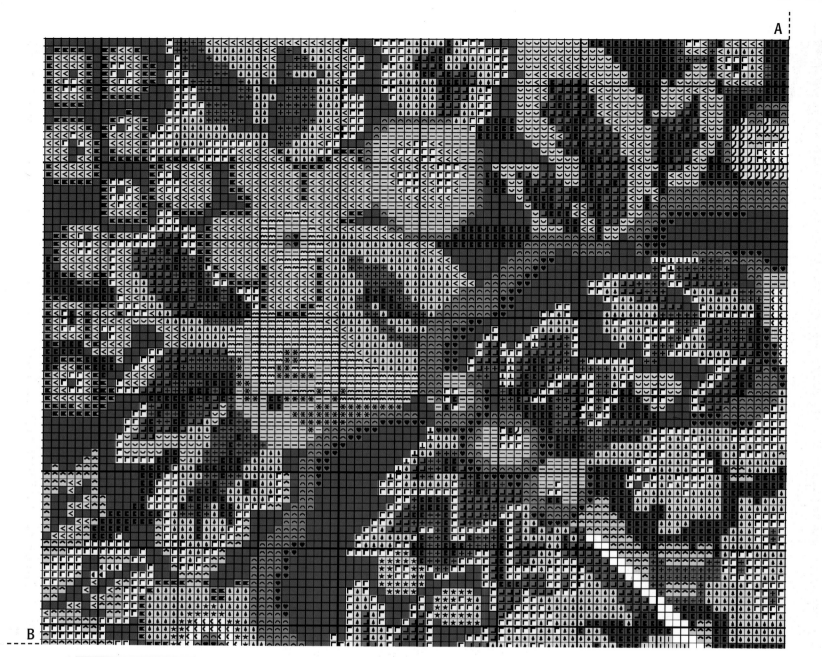

B

MATERIALS

14 mesh Mono canvas (cut size: 18 x 18")
Size 20 tapestry needle
26 shades Persian yarn (separate and use
only 1 strand of the 3-ply yarn)

195 stitches x 196 stitches

The design as shown was worked on 14
mesh canvas, using Erica Wilson Persian
yarn. To work on different sizes of mesh with
other yarns refer to the conversion chart on
p. 126.

Diagram for chart pp. 72–75:

<u>Note</u>: Using this diagram as a
guide, match up the letters and
the dotted lines showing where
the charts join. For instance, <u>A</u>
is at the edge of your first chart,
marked with a dotted line. On
the second chart, <u>A</u> is five
stitches in from the edge, also
marked with a dotted line. **This
is a five-stitch repeat which
should not be worked**–it is
there to help you establish your
position when continuing on to
the next chart.

A A

B

B

D

D

C C

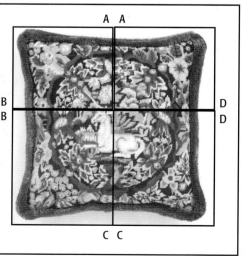

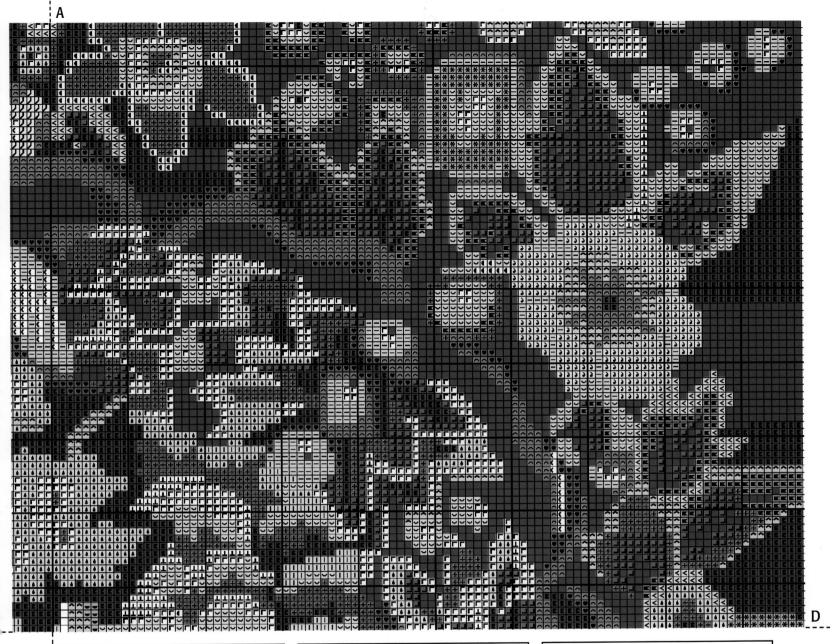

A

D

	Color #	Color (# of 3-ply 33" strands)
1.	EWP 5061	Dark Kelly Green (21)
2.	EWP 7021	Very Dark Blue Gn. (21)
3.	EWP 7033	Dark Green (5)
4.	EWP 5123	Dark Blue Green (14)
5.	EWP 5032	Bright Yellow Gn. (12)
6.	EWP 5035	Light Yellow Gn. (3)
7.	EWP 5066	Light Pistachio (14)
8.	EWP 5014	Medium Blue Green (14)
9.	EWP 5088	Medium Pistachio (18)

	Color #	Color
10.	EWP 5025	Light Gray Green (3)
11.	EWP 7026	Pale Powder Blue (4)
12.	EWP 7025	Palest Mint (3)
13.	EWP 5004	Dark Gray Green (7)
14.	EWP 4033	Dark Brass (2)
15.	EWP 4034	Medium Brass (7)
16.	EWP 5045	Light Green Tan (11)
17.	EWP 4015	Light Yellow (20)
18.	EWP 3004	Apricot (3)

	Color #	Color
19.	EWP 1010	Whipped Cream (3)
20.	EWP 2051	Dark Red (7)
21.	EWP 3043	True Red (10)
22.	EWP 3044	Dark Coral (7)
23.	EWP 3045	Medium Coral (7)
24.	EWP 3025	Pale Apricot (2)
25.	EWP 3026	Very Pale Apricot (6)
26.	EWP 3046	Light Coral (3)
27.	EWP 1001	White (4)

73

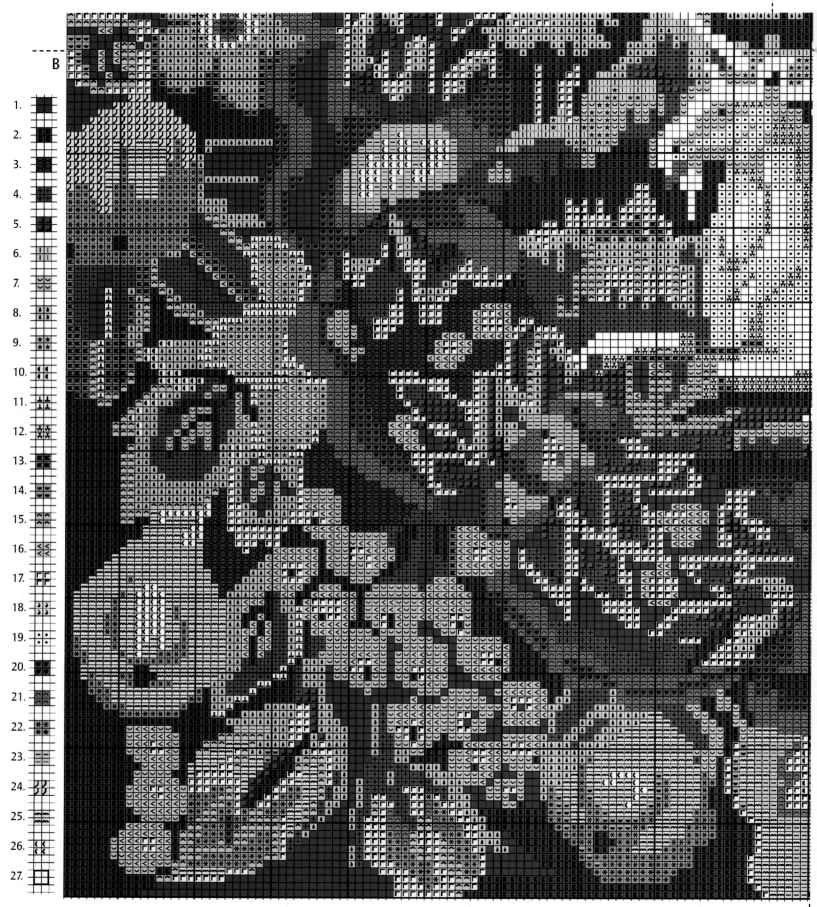

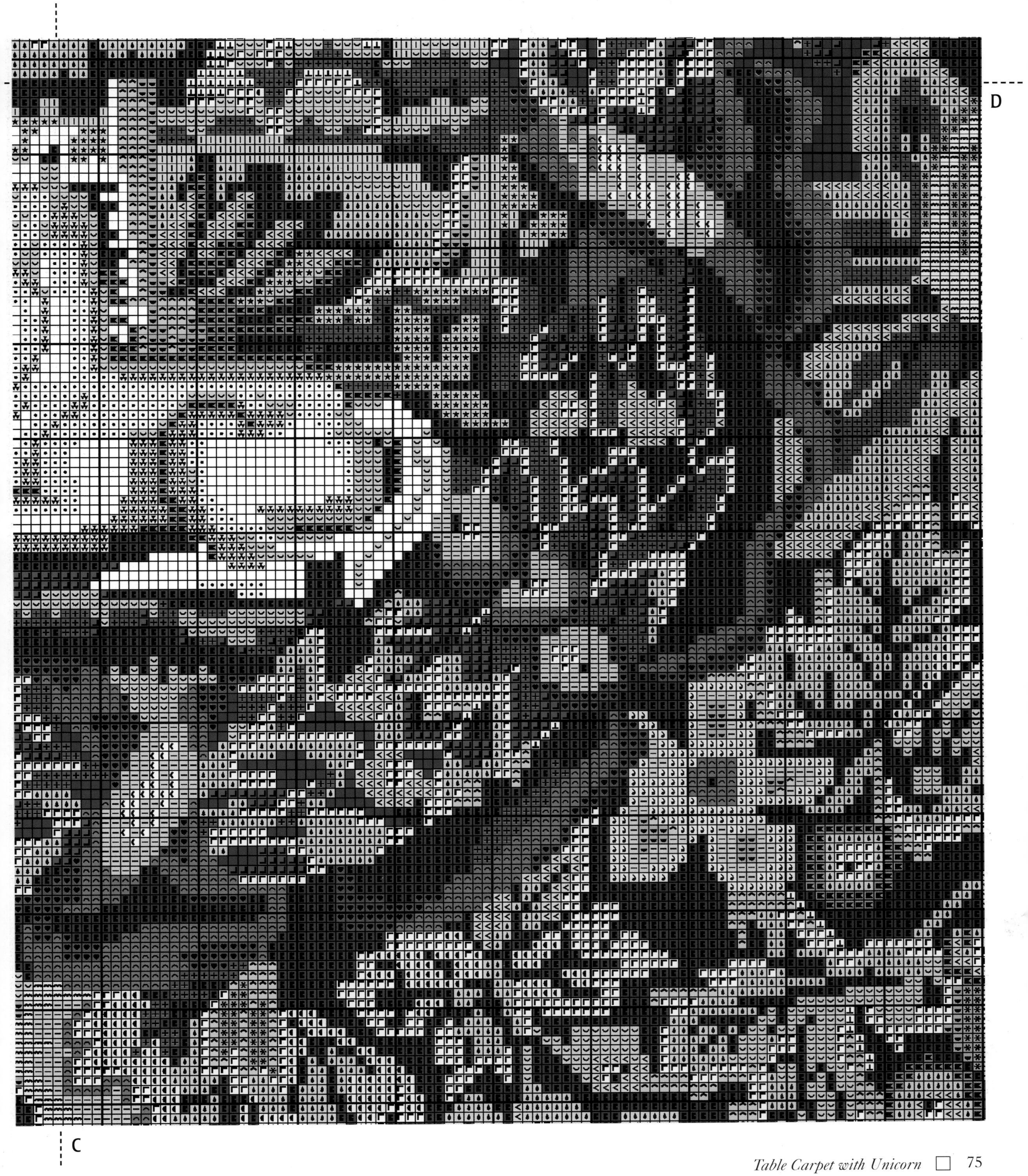
D
C

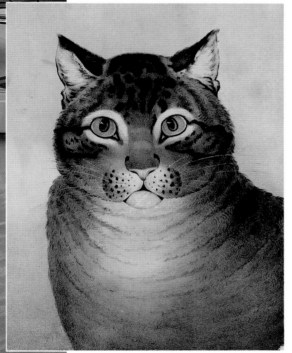

The Favorite Cat. Nathaniel Currier, publisher, American, active 1834–1857. Hand-colored lithograph, c.1840–50.

The Favorite Cat

Since prehistoric times, cats have been surrounded with an aura of mystery. By the nineteenth century, the cat was a popular subject in painting, sculpture, and needlework. During this time, Nathaniel Currier, of the well-known firm Currier & Ives, produced hand-colored lithographs that made color illustrations available inexpensively for the first time. This particular cat became one of the most successful subjects of Currier's print shop.

The cat's intense expression translates into a delightful needlepoint pillow worked in cotton floss. Or, if desired, you may exaggerate this expression even more by making a pillow showing only the cat's eyes and mouth on a fine mesh canvas, and framing the little pillow in black velvet. Simple colors and little shading make this "favorite cat" easy to interpret and satisfying to stitch.

A

B

MATERIALS

14 mesh Mono canvas (cut size: 17 x 17")
Size 20 tapestry needle
8 shades DMC floss (use all 6 strands of floss)

192 stitches x 187 stitches

The design as shown was worked on 14 mesh canvas, using DMC cotton floss. To work on different sizes of mesh with other yarns refer to the chart on p. 126.

Diagram for chart pp. 78–81:

Note: Using this diagram as a guide, match up the letters and the dotted lines showing where the charts join. For instance, **A** is at the edge of your first chart, marked with a dotted line. On the second chart, **A** is five stitches in from the edge, also marked with a dotted line. **This is a five-stitch repeat which should not be worked**–it is there to help you establish your position when continuing on to the next chart.

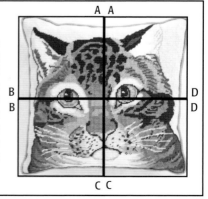

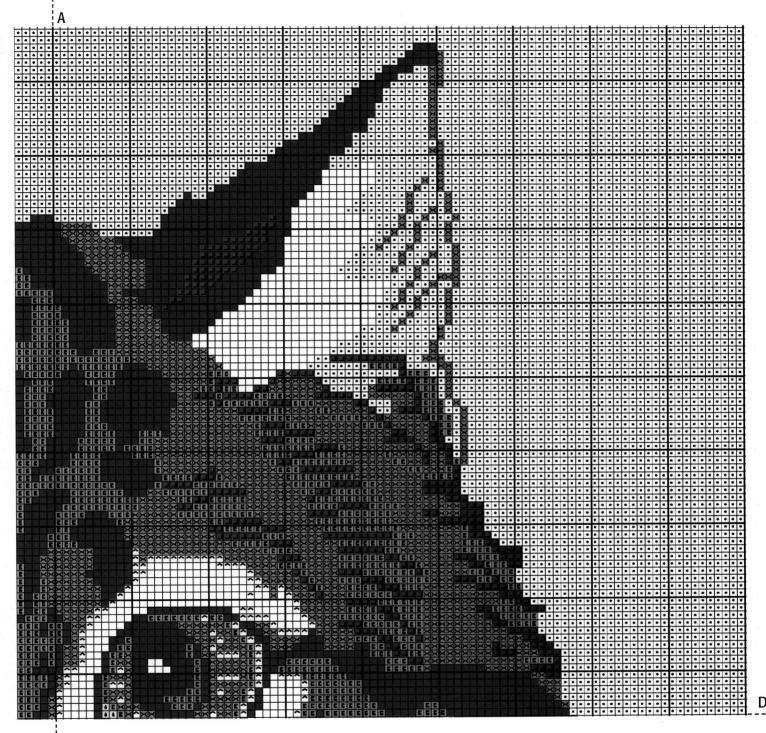

A

D

		Color #	Color (# of 9-yard skeins)
1.		DMC 310	Black (6)
2.		DMC 414	Silver Gray (7)
3.		DMC 415	Pearl Gray (6)
4.		DMC 413	Slate Gray (5)

		Color #	Color (# of 9-yard skeins)
5.		DMC 676	Chamois (1)
6.		DMC 822	Cream (2)
7.		DMC Ecru	Ecru (13)
8.		DMC White	White (6)

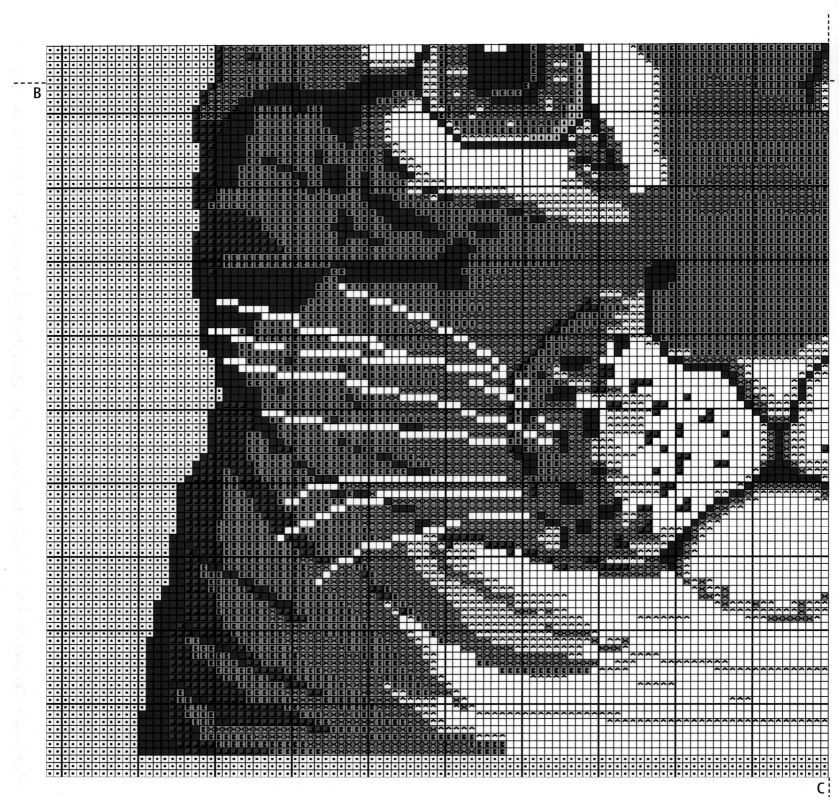

B

C

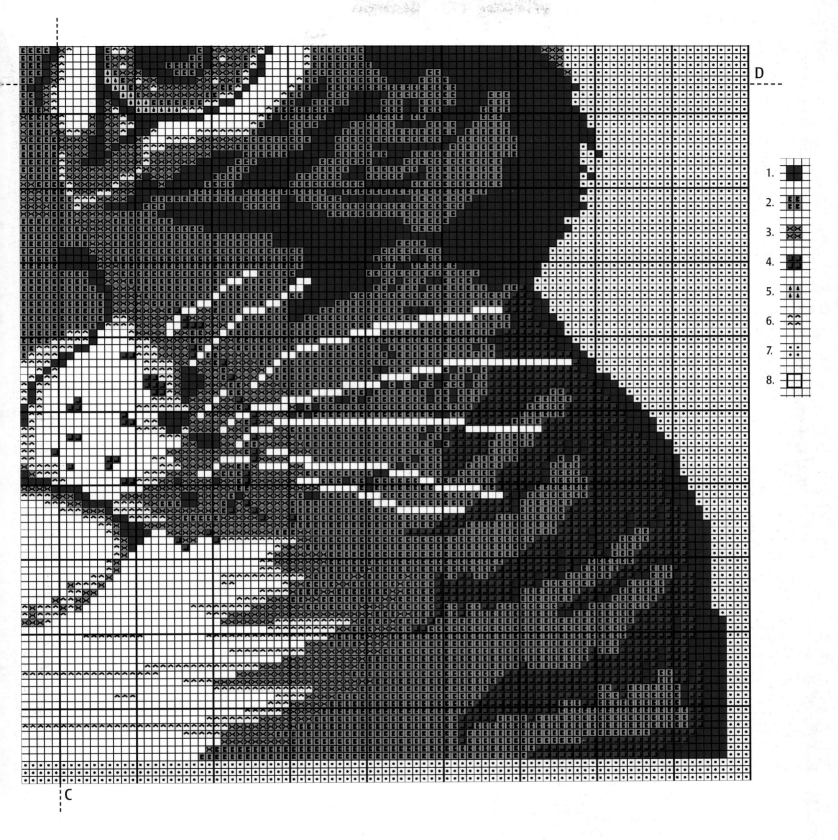

D

C

Still Life: Flowers and Fruit.
Severin Roesen, German,
active in America 1848–1872.
Oil on canvas, 1850–55.

Severin Roesen Flowers

Severin Roesen's still life paintings are filled with glowing colors, translucent fruits, dewdrops, bird's nests, and full-blown flowers. Born near Cologne, Germany, Roesen emigrated to New York in 1848, moved on to Philadelphia and finally settled in Williamsport, Pennsylvania. Having started life as a porcelain and enamel painter, his training stood him in good stead as he found fertile ground for his creative powers in North America.

Severin Roesen's still lifes, with their technical brilliance and meticulous detail, are particularly suited to needlepoint. Each color is separate and distinct, yet blends realistically into a harmonious whole. The pillows shown here are adapted from different areas in the painting and could easily be used as squares to form a rug. The rich glowing colors and dramatic highlights make this an exciting design to work, especially when you set off the colors with a dark background.

When choosing colors, be sure to group them in shadings for each flower and fruit, then lay them on top of a large bundle of the background shade. Lay all the colors on the floor and stand back so that you can get the effect from a distance. Then, if necessary, change and rearrange the colors until the shades are harmonious and balanced.

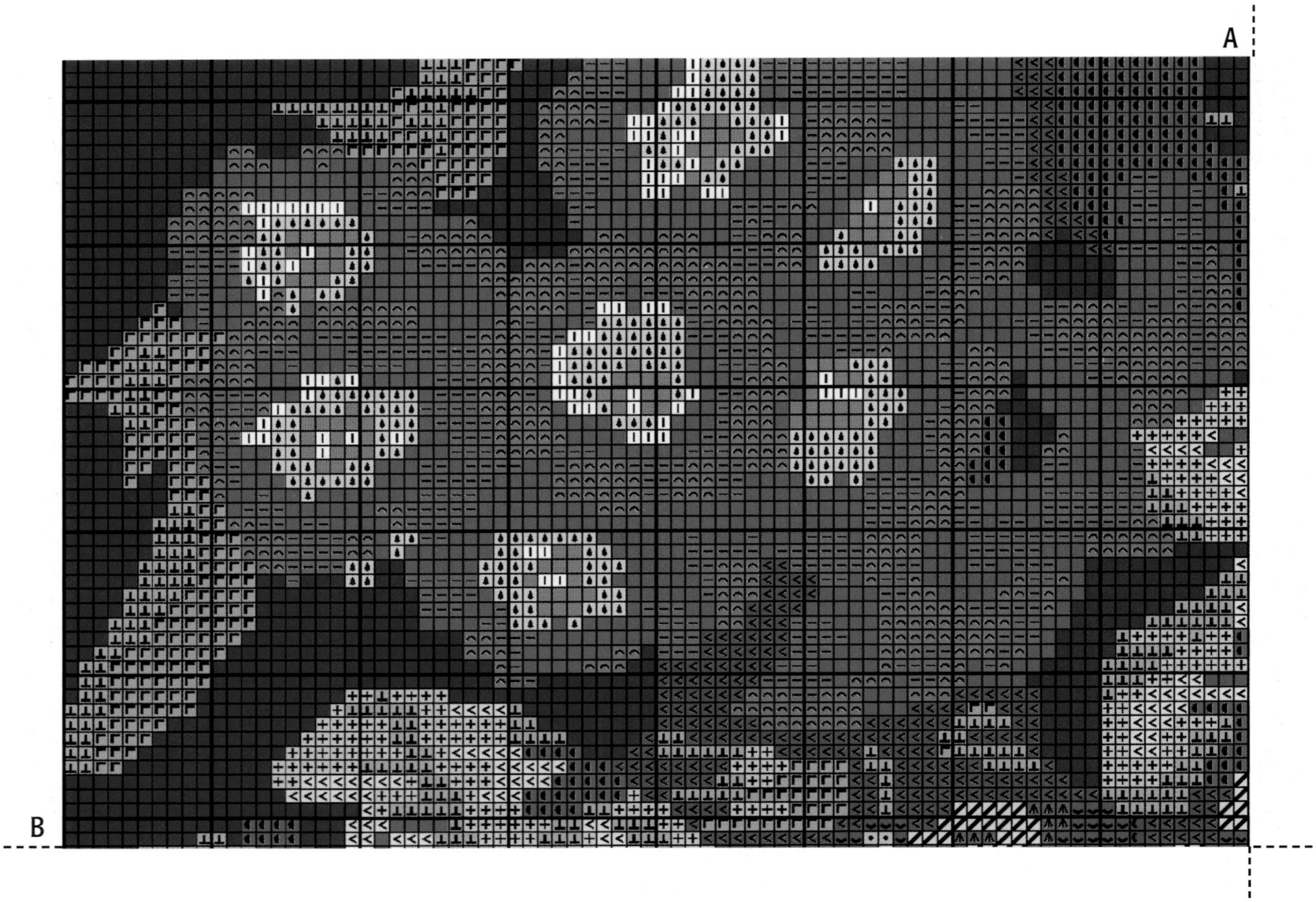

MATERIALS

10 mesh Mono canvas (cut size: 20 x 20")
Size 18 tapestry needle
25 shades Persian yarn (use all 3 strands of yarn)

162 stitches x 160 stitches

The design as shown was worked on 10 mesh canvas, using Erica Wilson Persian yarn. To work on different sizes of mesh with other yarns refer to the chart on p.126.

Diagram for chart pp. 84–87:

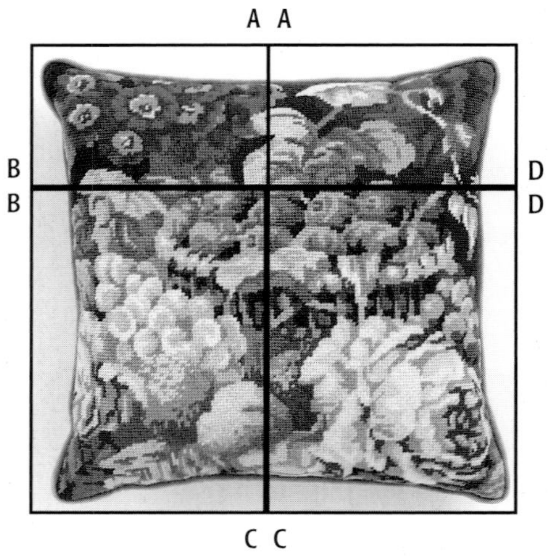

Note: Using this diagram as a guide, match up the letters and the dotted lines showing where the charts join. For instance, A is at the edge of your first chart, marked with a dotted line. On the second chart, A is five stitches in from the edge, also marked with a dotted line. **This is a five-stitch repeat which should not be worked**—it is there to help you establish your position when continuing on to the next chart.

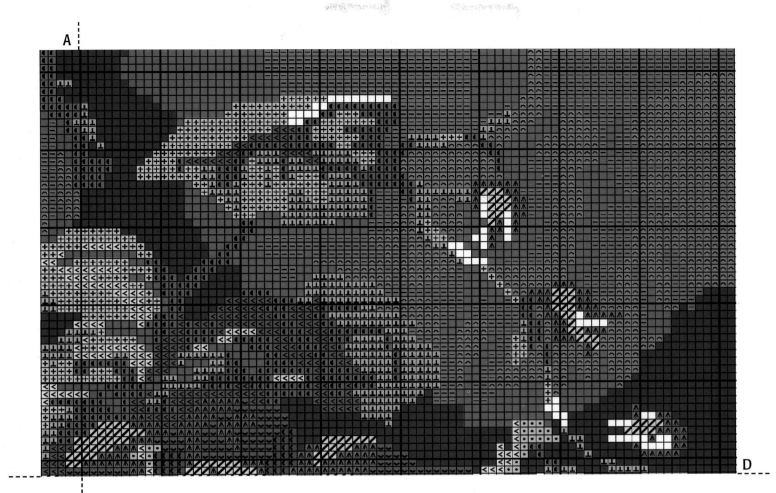

A | D

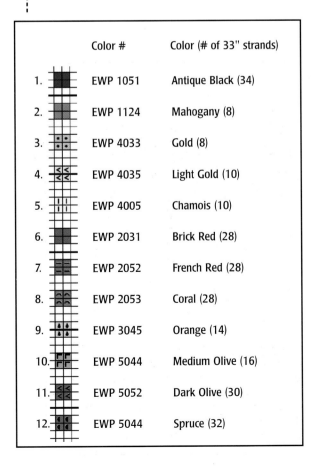

		Color #	Color (# of 33" strands)
1.		EWP 1051	Antique Black (34)
2.		EWP 1124	Mahogany (8)
3.		EWP 4033	Gold (8)
4.		EWP 4035	Light Gold (10)
5.		EWP 4005	Chamois (10)
6.		EWP 2031	Brick Red (28)
7.		EWP 2052	French Red (28)
8.		EWP 2053	Coral (28)
9.		EWP 3045	Orange (14)
10.		EWP 5044	Medium Olive (16)
11.		EWP 5052	Dark Olive (30)
12.		EWP 5044	Spruce (32)

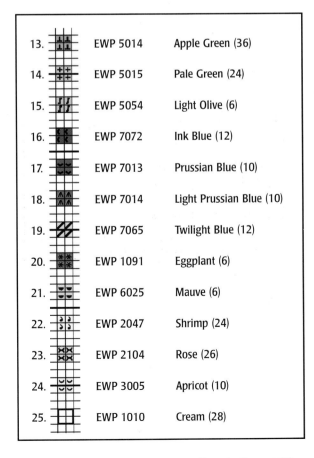

13.		EWP 5014	Apple Green (36)
14.		EWP 5015	Pale Green (24)
15.		EWP 5054	Light Olive (6)
16.		EWP 7072	Ink Blue (12)
17.		EWP 7013	Prussian Blue (10)
18.		EWP 7014	Light Prussian Blue (10)
19.		EWP 7065	Twilight Blue (12)
20.		EWP 1091	Eggplant (6)
21.		EWP 6025	Mauve (6)
22.		EWP 2047	Shrimp (24)
23.		EWP 2104	Rose (26)
24.		EWP 3005	Apricot (10)
25.		EWP 1010	Cream (28)

B

C

Caswell Carpet

The Caswell Carpet.
Zeruah Higley Guernsey
Caswell, American, 19th
century. Embroidered in
colored woolen yarns on
twill-weave woolen fabric,
1832–35. GIFT OF KATHERINE
KEYES, IN MEMORY OF HER FATHER,
HOMER EATON KEYES, 1938

With its early American design, marvelous use of color, and charming simplicity, the Caswell Carpet is a remarkable example of nineteenth-century needlework. Its creator, Zeruah Higley Guernsey Caswell from Castleton, Vermont, was responsible for every step in the carpet's production: she sheared the sheep, spun and dyed the yarn, and wove the fabric. Finally she embroidered the homespun with a wooden needle, stitching all but two of the squares herself. The entire carpet was completed in less than three years, an amazing feat considering it has 76 squares, with one large removable panel. The panel features a handsome basket overflowing with grapes and other fruits, with curving tendrils bearing leaves and flowers on either side. The section that lays closest to the hearth was designed to be taken away in the summer, and laid over the empty hearth.

The removable panel from the Caswell Carpet makes a natural area rug. Because the design is like a stencil, it may be worked easily on the bold mesh of a number seven canvas. Cut the canvas with at least four inches extra on all sides, since the large mesh frays more easily and blocking the finished rug requires a wide border.

The basket with stylized grapes would also make an interesting fireboard. The basket could be worked on ten mesh canvas, then the whole design could be cut out around the shape, and backed on padded plywood to stand in the fireplace, like the one on p. 18.

MATERIALS

8 mesh Mono canvas (cut size: 45 x 32")
Size 16 tapestry needle
24 shades Persian yarn (use all 3 strands of
the 3-ply yarn)

340 stitches x 170 stitches

The design as shown was worked on 8 mesh
canvas using Erica Wilson Persian yarn. To
work on different sizes of mesh with other
yarns refer to the chart on p. 126.

Diagram for chart pp. 90–95:

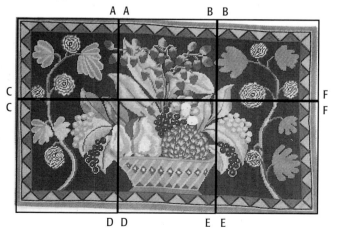

Note: Using this diagram as a guide, match up the letters and the dotted lines showing where
the charts join. For instance, **A** is at the edge of your first chart, marked with a dotted line.
On the second chart, **A** is five stitches in from the edge, also marked with a dotted line. **This
is a five-stitch repeat which should not be worked**–it is there to help you establish your
position when continuing on to the next chart.

A   B

	Color #	Color (# of 3-ply 33" strands)
1.	EWP 1122	Dark Brown (180)
2.	EWP 1162	Medium Brown (15)
3.	EWP 1113	Mustard Brown (15)
4.	EWP 4034	Gold (9)
5.	EWP 4055	Pale Gold (18)
6.	EWP 4057	Cream (50)
7.	EWP 4063	Yellow (20)
8.	EWP 2021	Eggplant (46)

9.	EWP 3071	Rust (40)
10.	EWP 3041	Strawberry Red (46)
11.	EWP 2044	Coral (17)
12.	EWP 2033	Ash Rose (60)
13.	EWP 3085	Dusty Apricot (46)
14.	EWP 2104	Dusty Rose (80)
15.	EWP 2047	Pale Pink (25)
16.	EWP 3075	Dusty Peach (50)

17.	EWP 7072	Navy Blue (15)
18.	EWP 7024	Sea Foam Green (15)
19.	EWP 7026	Pale Sea Foam Green (16)
20.	EWP 1143	Khaki (5)
21.	EWP 5066	Moss Green (12)
22.	EWP 5067	Pale Moss Green (7)
23.	EWP 1213	Pale Mauve (12)
24.	EWP 1222	Palest Mauve (90)

1. ■
2. ■
3. ■
4. ■
5. ■
6. ■
7. ■
8. ■
9. ■
10. ■
11. ■
12. ■
13. ■
14. ■
15. ■
16. ■
17. ■
18. ■
19. ■
20. ■
21. ■
22. ■
23. ■
24. ■

B

F

C

D

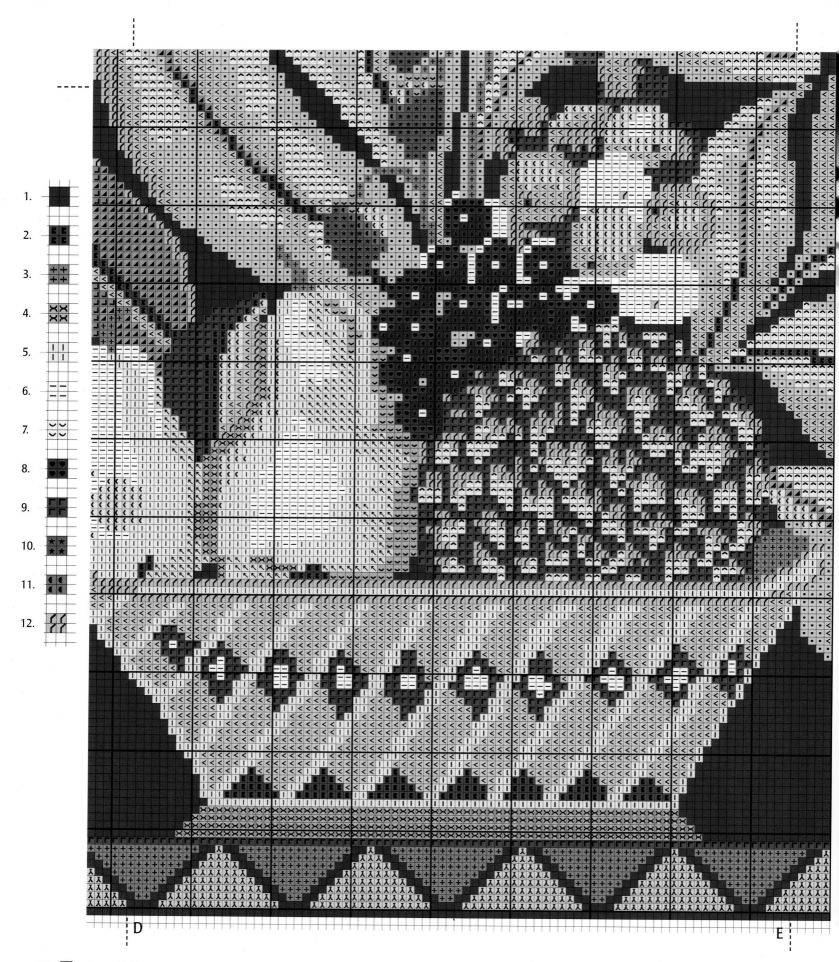

1.
2.
3.
4.
5.
6.
7.
8.
9.
10.
11.
12.

D

E

13.
14.
15.
16.
17.
18.
19.
20.
21.
22.
23.
24.

Wall Panel. French, about 1700.
Silk embroidery on canvas.
PURCHASE, GIFT OF ADELE PHARO AZAR,
IN MEMORY OF HER HUSBAND, JEMILE
WEHBY AZAR, BY EXCHANGE, 1987

France and Italy became the European centers for the manufacture of silk embroidery and weaving in the seventeenth and eighteenth centuries. Large hangings for secular and ecclesiastical use were designed, and long stitches which showed the sheen of the precious thread on the surface, such as crewel embroidery, were used frequently.

This beautiful silk embroidered wall hanging dated about 1700 uses silks on canvas with crewel embroidery. Woven patterns with the lights and darks of flowing acanthus leaves are combined symmetrically with strapwork, arabesques, and flourishes. Elaborate fountains with sea horses, dolphins, and peacocks intertwine with foliage and fruits that blend into one shimmering panel of gold, apricot, and rose.

Because of the bold scale of the design, this needlepoint may be interpreted on large mesh canvas. The pillow is on twelve mesh canvas, and it could be extended even further with a velvet border and silk fringe, or used to cover a large square stool. The Christmas stocking is on fourteen mesh, and the richness of the colors is accented by a peacock blue velvet mounting. At the top of the stocking is an open panel that could be stitched with the recipient's name. This design would also be excellent as a set of dining room chair seats. The leaves and strapwork could be adapted into a formal architectural framework to encircle the fruits and birds, and this centerpiece could be slightly changed on each seat to make each unique, yet part of a set. The autumn coloring and soft shading of the fruits, flowers, and birds make this design suitable for any room.

MATERIALS

12 mesh Mono canvas (cut size: 22 x 22")
Size 18 tapestry needle
27 shades Persian yarn (separate and use only
    2 strands of the 3-ply yarn)

211 stitches x 207 stitches

The design as shown was worked on 12 mesh
canvas, using Erica Wilson Persian yarn. To work
on different sizes of mesh with other yarns refer
to the chart on p. 126.

Diagram for chart pp. 98–103:

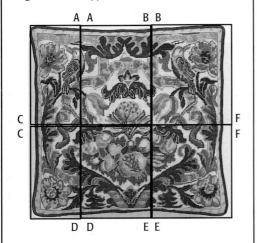

Note: Using this diagram as a guide, match up the letters
and the dotted lines showing where the charts join.
For instance, <u>A</u> is at the edge of your first chart, marked
with a dotted line. On the second chart, <u>A</u> is five stitches
in from the edge, also marked with a dotted line. **This
is a five-stitch repeat which should not be worked—**
it is there to help you establish your position when
continuing on to the next chart.

	Color #	Color (# of 3-ply 33" strands)
1.	EWP 7011	Deep Blue (11)
2.	EWP 7003	Williamsburg Blue (18)
3.	EWP 7004	Pale Williamsburg Blue (17)
4.	EWP 7005	Prussian Blue (17)
5.	EWP 7006	Pale Prussian Blue (6)
6.	EWP 7008	Palest Prussian Blue (28)
7.	EWP 5062	Hunter Green (96)

A   B

	Color #	Color (# of 3-ply 33" strands)
8.	EWP 5066	Mint Green (7)
9.	EWP 5005	Sage Green (8)
10.	EWP 4032	Tan (2)
11.	EWP 5092	Olive Green (24)
12.	EWP 2031	Brick Red (28)
13.	EWP 2032	Faded Red (11)
14.	EWP 1186	Dusty Rose (18)
15.	EWP 3006	Pale Peach (24)
16.	EWP 1212	Dark Mauve (27)
17.	EWP 1213	Medium Mauve (18)
18.	EWP 1214	Pale Mauve (11)
19.	EWP 4036	Pale Yellow (65)
20.	EWP 1111	Dark Chocolate Brown (12)
21.	EWP 4031	Brown (15)
22.	EWP 4023	Apricot Gold (35)
23.	EWP 4052	Gold (45)
24.	EWP 1144	Beige (6)
25.	EWP 4034	Antique Yellow (8)
26.	EWP 4033	Dark Gold (30)
27.	EWP 1010	Cream (130)

B

F

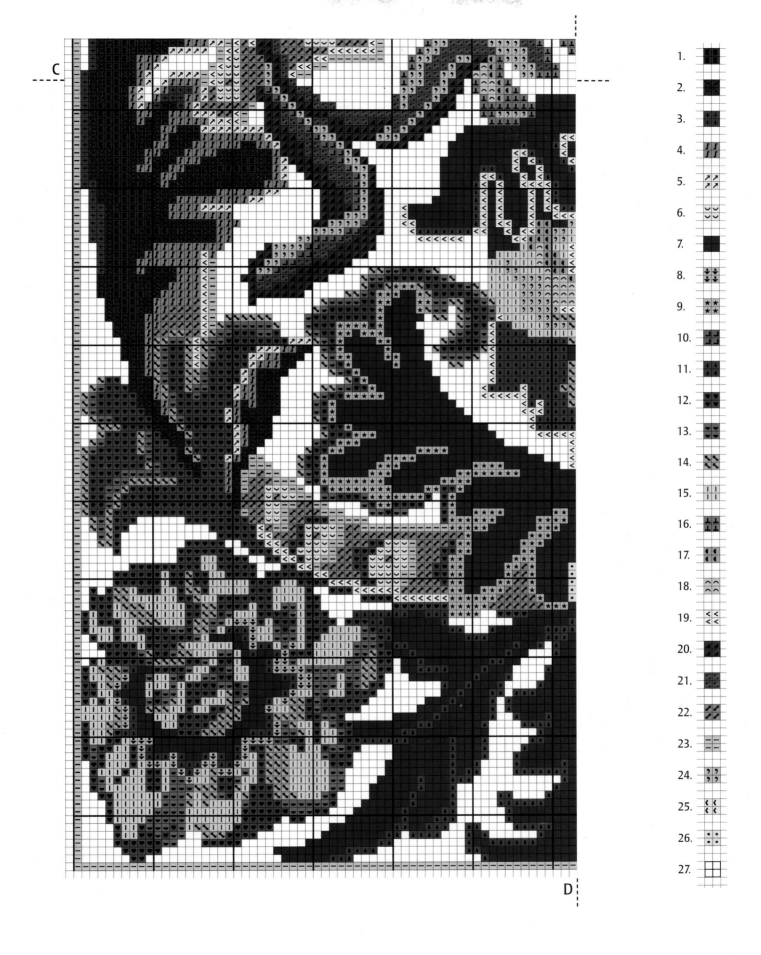

Tobacco Leaf

The Tobacco Leaf design that features a flowering nicotiana plant is one of the many decorative patterns the Europeans provided to Chinese merchants for reproduction in porcelain. Although the origin of the Tobacco Leaf pattern is unknown, its bright colors and shapes have parallels in porcelain designs developed around 1780 for the Portuguese market.

The Tobacco Leaf pattern, probably made for bulk shipments to Europe, exists in a number of different versions. The bird is omitted altogether in some patterns and others boast an entirely different arrangement of leaves and flowers. The silhouette of flowers and leaves lend themselves perfectly to needlepoint and the touches of real gold metal thread give this design an extra touch of elegance.

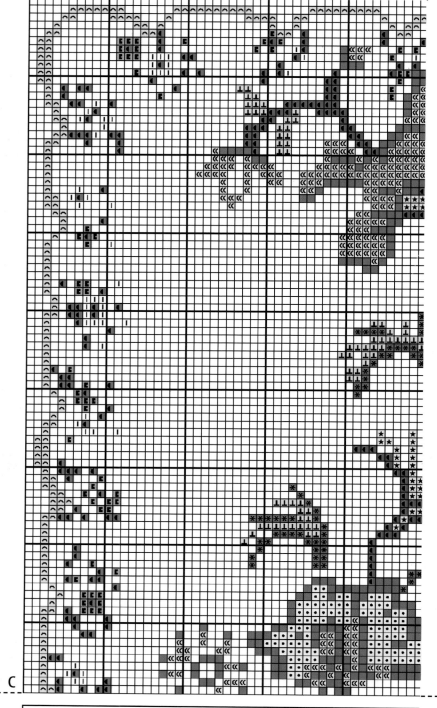

A

C

	Color #	Color (# of 33" strands)
1.	EWP 2048	Light Pink (6)
2.	EWP 2047	Shrimp (4)
3.	EWP 2015	Dusty Rose (8)
4.	EWP 2006	Dark Dusty Rose (4)
5.	EWP 3045	Apricot (4)
6.	EWP 3044	Orange (6)
7.	EWP 2072	French Red (9)
8.	Metallic Gold	Metallic Gold (35)
9.	EWP 4015	Butter Yellow (3)
10.	EWP 4063	Canary Yellow (11)
11.	EWP 4072	Gold (3)
12.	EWP 5036	Key Lime Green (3)
13.	EWP 5023	Apple Green (6)
14.	EWP 7095	Mint (9)
15.	EWP 5067	Light Mint (9)
16.	EWP 7093	Turquoise (15)
17.	EWP 7007	Light Sky Blue (5)
18.	EWP 7054	Heron Blue (7)
19.	EWP 7053	Blue Azure (9)
20.	EWP 7052	Blueberry (7)
21.	EWP 1001	Snow White (45)

Diagram for chart pp. 106–11:

Note: Using this diagram as a guide, match up the letters and the dotted lines showing where the charts join. For instance, A is at the edge of your first chart, marked with a dotted line. On the second chart, A is five stitches in from the edge, also marked with a dotted line. **This is a five-stitch repeat which should not be worked**—it is there to help you establish your position when continuing on to the next chart.

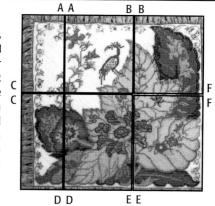

A A   B B

C

C

F

F

D D   E E

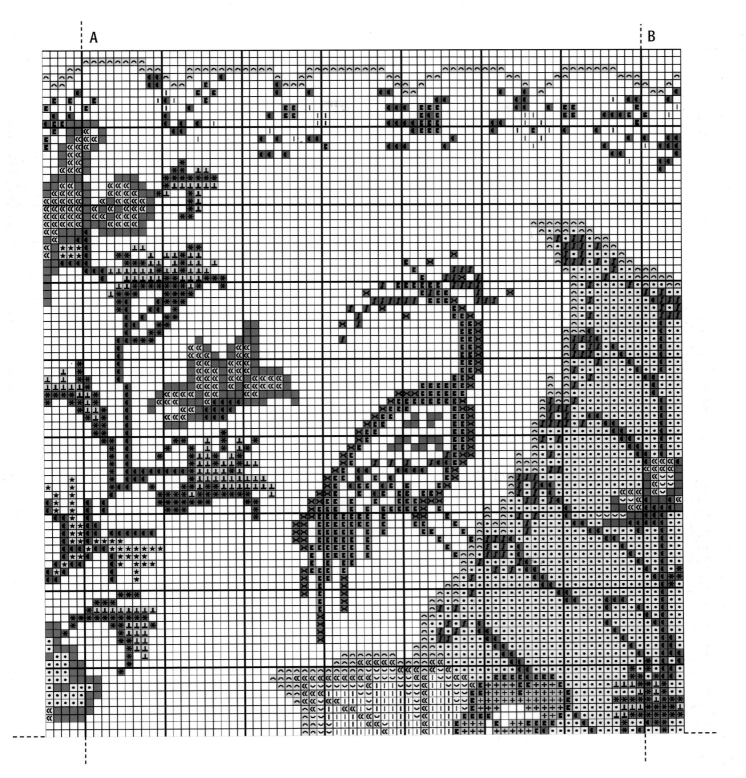

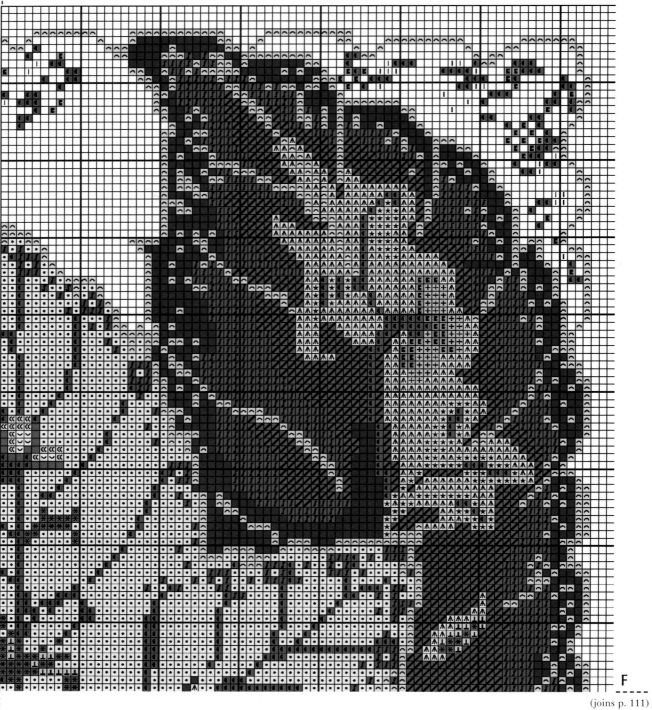

F

(joins p. 111)

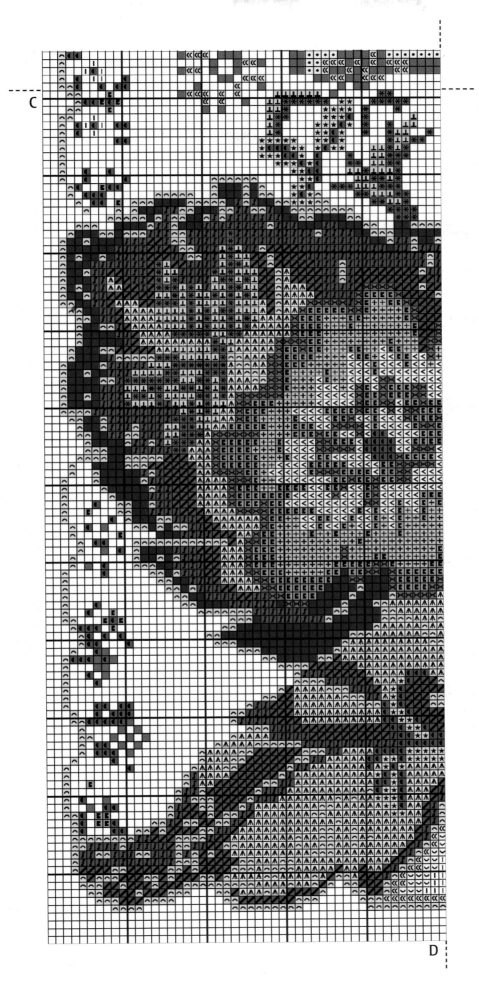
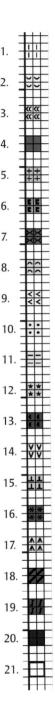

C

D

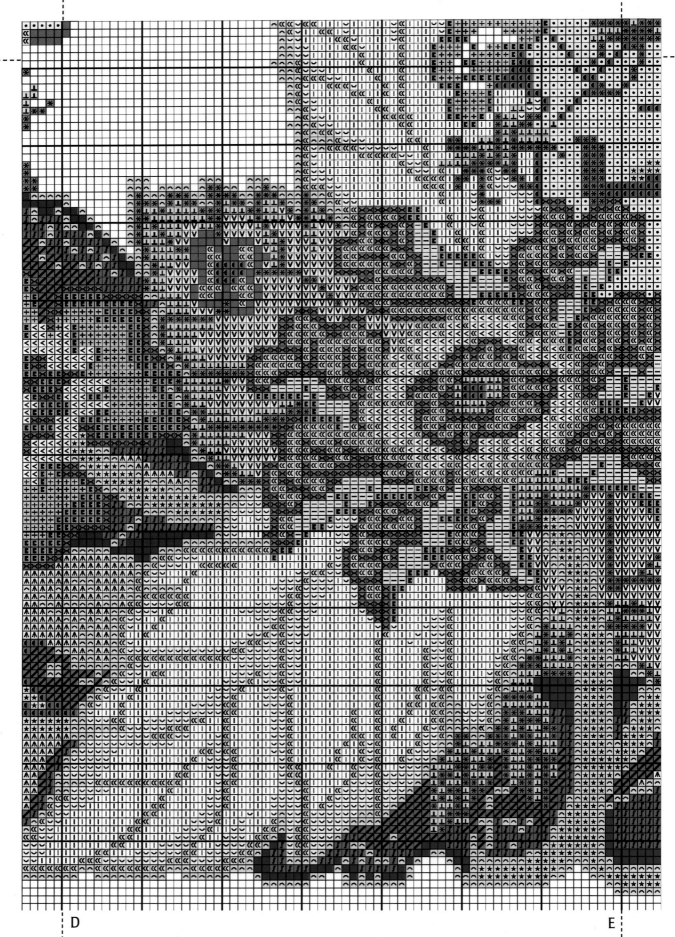

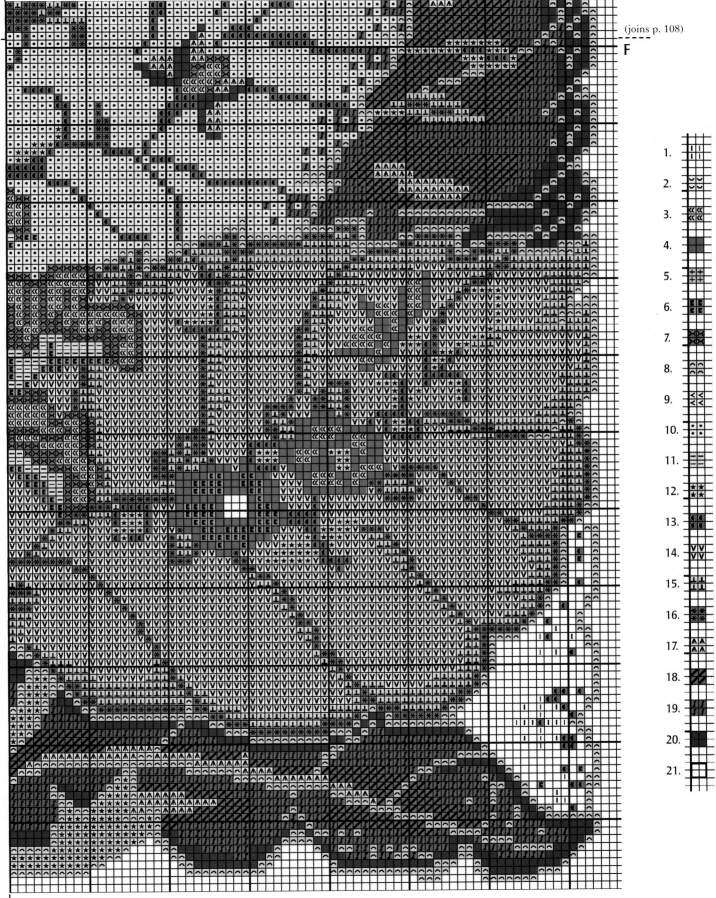

(joins p. 108)

F

1.
2.
3.
4.
5.
6.
7.
8.
9.
10.
11.
12.
13.
14.
15.
16.
17.
18.
19.
20.
21.

E

General Instructions

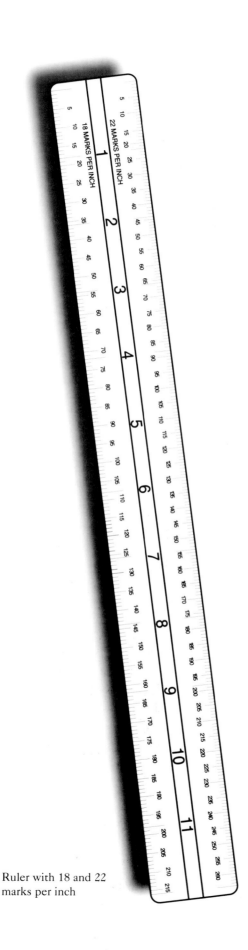

Ruler with 18 and 22
marks per inch

MATERIALS

The first thing you need to buy, naturally, is canvas. How do you know what to choose? There are three basic types: Mono, Interlock, and Penelope. Mono is an evenly woven canvas, usually white, and excellent for marking out designs clearly. Interlock has two double threads woven together (like its name). Because the two threads are so finely interwoven, the canvas does not shift and it holds its shape well. The third type of canvas is called Penelope, which is woven with separated double threads. This gives more strength to a bold weave, so Penelope is excellent for rugs on #5 or #7 mesh, for instance.

For most of the projects in this book, Mono or Interlock will be what you need. Always buy good quality canvas, watch for slubs and flaws, and make sure it is neither too limp nor too stiff or scratchy. Buy enough canvas to allow the selvage to run vertically on either side of the design you have chosen, to ensure better wear.

Wools come very fine: English yarn; very bold: tapestry yarn; and halfway between: Persian three-stranded yarn. Of all the yarns, Persian is the most versatile because the three strands are lightly twisted together to form one thread. All of the designs in this book have been worked with Erica Wilson's Persian-type yarn. These can be separated and used in one, two, three, or more strands, according to the mesh size you are using. (See chart on p. 126, suppliers p. 128.)

Cotton floss, or mercerized cotton looks just like silk but wears better. It comes in six-stranded skeins which may be separated or doubled to fit the canvas (see chart p. 126). Perle cotton is a shiny twist in two thicknesses (no. 5 and no. 3), and gold lurex thread called fil d'or is a nontarnishing thread you can sew with.

Needles are very important. Tapestry needles have long eyes to carry the wool easily and blunt points to glide smoothly between the threads of the canvas. The needle should be large enough to protect the thread as it passes through without having to push too hard (see chart p. 126). The needle must also be of good quality—the inside of the eye is ground finely so that it does not tear the yarn.

Materials you will need:

canvas (see each chart for amounts)
yarn (see each chart for amounts)
tapestry needle
embroidery frame (optional)
scissors
hard pencil (3H) or Trace Erase pen
eraser
ruler
masking or artist's tape for binding canvas

COLORS

Each color used in the design is shown in a numbered block at the side of each graph. You may not always be able to match the shades exactly, so as you pick, notice how the colors blend with one another, and pick with the end result in sight rather than trying to get an identical match to every individual color. Instead of sticking to the shades provided by the dyer in each range of color, you can also make up your own combinations, picking dark, medium, and light shades from different color ranges. For instance, if you are working with light, medium, and dark lavender blue, you might get a lively effect by substituting a medium turquoise between the light and the dark. When you gather all your yarns, look at them for an overall effect. If they blend nicely together, they will also look beautiful in the design. Don't be afraid of brilliant colors; they never look as bright when they are worked as they do in the skein. Conversely, if you are working with earth tones and muted shades, be careful not to add too many bright accents, to throw the whole design off balance.

Many of the square blocks of the graphs have printed symbols as well as colors. This makes each color easy to recognize when it occurs in another area; i.e, the same pink may look entirely different when it is juxtaposed to another color in another place on the design, so the symbol helps to make it distinguishable. As a guide, you may tape a few threads of each color next to each color block. This makes a "shade card" to help you use the charts. Note: <u>The colors in the charts do not always agree with the colors in the finished piece.</u> The charts were designed this way so that when you're counting each stitch you can differentiate between the shades more easily.

DESIGN SIZES

Each design is shown with its number of stitches listed beside it. Only the number of stitches is given, not the measurement in inches, because the size will vary depending upon the canvas mesh size you decide to work on. On pages 114–15 you will find a useful ruler with the inch equivalent of the number of stitches in different sizes of mesh. First count the number of stitches in the design, then decide on the mesh size, and finally arrive at the measurement of your finished piece by checking the ruler. Once you have decided on the design and its size, you are ready to buy your materials. Always buy sufficient canvas to allow for at least a four-inch border all around the design to allow for turn backs. You can always trim, but never add, without a great deal of difficulty! Also, always buy a little more yarn than you think; you may need to allow for mistakes. You may find it hard to match a dye-lot once you have run out of a color. If you do think you may run out, save enough thread of the original color to mix with the new shade. Work with both together in the needle to make a smooth transition, this way the old and new shades should blend less noticeably. If you are working with a single thread, work a little of the

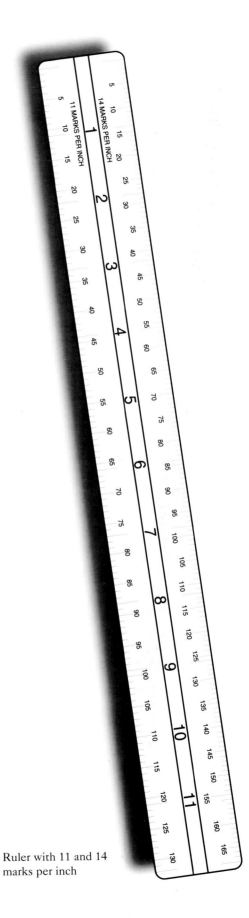

Ruler with 11 and 14 marks per inch

old and a little of the new in long and short rows together to achieve the same blending effect.

WORKING FROM THE GRAPHS

Each design in this book has been transposed onto a square grid to resemble the canvas, and each square equals one stitch.

When working from one chart to the other, you will notice a five-stitch repeat. This repeat should not be worked—it is there to help you establish your position when continuing on to the next chart.

Each chart has been drawn with bolder lines every ten squares. You can mark your canvas the same way. To do this fold the canvas in half in one direction, then in half in the other direction. Crease it firmly, open it up, and you will be able to establish the center point where the creases intersect. Now, find the center point of your graph, and count the number of squares from the center out to any one of the four sides. Count the same number on your canvas, from the center to one of the outer edges. Then repeat this on the other three sides of the design. You will now be able to outline your design with a fine line on all four sides. Now count and mark off every ten threads along the bottom and one side of the design (it is quicker to count in pairs of threads). Once you have marked two sides you can extend the lines right through the design in both directions and you will have formed a mesh of squares to use as your pattern guide.

A word of warning: Mark these squares and outlines *very lightly,* so that you can barely see them, using a no. 3H (very hard) pencil. If you pull the pencil *lightly* between the threads of the canvas, it will stay in the grooves, and you will not need a ruler. Never use a ballpoint pen, as the ink will run when you block your finished piece. Never use a permanent marker; you will not be able to cover the lines, particularly with light colored wools. Never use a soft pencil; it will make your wool look dirty. You may, however, use a Trace Erase pen (see suppliers, p. 128) instead of a hard pencil, because the ink will disappear with cold water. If a blue cloud appears when dry, simply dampen the work again until it is permanently clean. Never apply heat before the ink is removed, for it may set the blue lines permanently.

Now that your canvas is prepared, you are ready to start stitching the design. *Important:* When counting the design out on the canvas, always count the THREADS and *never* the holes. This avoids the confusion of counting the threads and other times the holes.

You can follow the graphs in many different ways. Some people prefer to start in the center and work out, counting each individual shape and completing one color before going to the next. Others prefer to stitch by row, working down from the top or up from the bottom. Alternatively, you can work each individual block of ten squares, adding them like building blocks, until the design area is built up and all that remains is the background area. Working such a small area makes it easier to check for accuracy as you go along.

If you are working on a frame, it is easier to thread several needles with different colors, leaving them hanging on the front, ready to be picked up and used as you need them. Do not end off the colors in each block as you complete it; bring them to the front ready to be used in each successive block as you work. However, never jump many more than six threads on the reverse side, for you will leave too long a thread that might catch and pucker the work. Instead, end the color off and start it off again where you need it.

CHOOSING A FRAME

Frames have been used since medieval days by professionals and in workshops, because they make the needlepoint faster and smoother, and the outlines and shading more accurate. The stitches worked in a frame are so even, the finished piece hardly needs blocking.

A frame stretches the canvas flat out like a board, so you can count the threads more easily. As you work, you can see how the stitches line up with one another, and can run the needle along the threads of the canvas to check this. You can also work with several needles threaded with different colors and leave them hanging on the front of the frame to use as you need them.

There are many different types of frames to choose from. The types of frames are:

A. Standing floor frame
B. Portable lap frame
C. Embroidery hoop frame
D. Artists' stretcher frame
E. Oval rug frame
F. Square frame

A *square* frame in which the canvas can be rolled up on one side and unrolled on the other as the work progresses is excellent for needlepoint because it holds the mesh square and taut. The main disadvantage of the square frame is that it is awkward to move about. Secondly it will only take material of the same width as itself. The length may be rolled around the rollers, but the width can only be that of the frame, 18 inches, 24 inches, or 36 inches (average frame sizes). So it is impossible to work a large rug without having the frame made up to a special size. This is where a *hoop* frame that just stretches the area on which you are working is especially useful. Needlepoint canvas is tough and resilient and

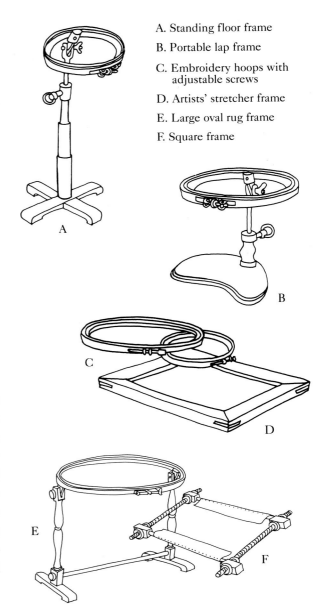

A. Standing floor frame

B. Portable lap frame

C. Embroidery hoops with adjustable screws

D. Artists' stretcher frame

E. Large oval rug frame

F. Square frame

117

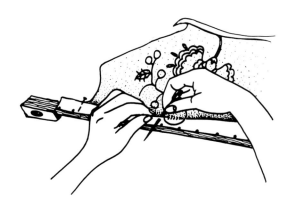

MOUNTING WORK IN A SQUARE FRAME

First stitch the fabric to the webbing of the square frame.

Then stretch tight, stitch webbing to either side and lace tightly with string as shown at right.

MOUNTING WORK IN A RING HOOP

Before assembling the frame, adjust the screw so that the outer hoop fits snugly over the inner ring and the material. Never try to alter the screw when the frame is in place.

Pull the material taut; if the upper ring is tight enough the material will not slip back.

When the material is taut, push the upper ring down. To release the fabric do not unscrew the frame, but press thumbs down firmly into the fabric on the frame, at the same time lifting off the outer ring.

On any frame always stab up and down, never "sew." Work with both hands, keeping one always below the frame and the other above. This becomes much easier with practice and is essential for speed and dexterity.

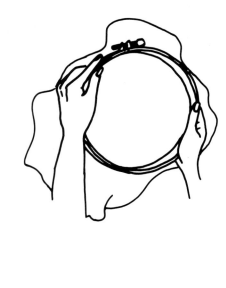

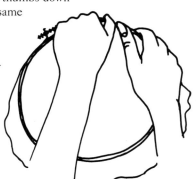

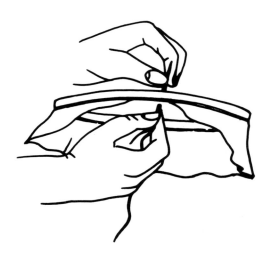

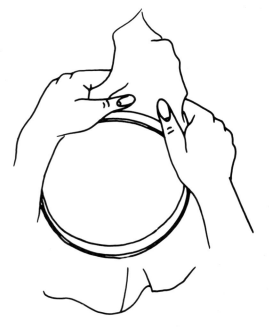

never gets damaged by having hoops pushed over it. But when stretching the canvas in a hoop frame, be sure to pull the opposite sides against one another, not the diagonals, or you may pull the mesh out of shape.

Another choice is to work on a *stretcher* frame. Artists' stretcher frames, used for painting on canvas, come in all sizes and are available at most art supply stores. You should buy a slightly larger size frame than the finished measurement of your work to allow you to work right up to the edge of the design without the wooden stretchers getting in the way. Assemble the four stretchers and pull your material tightly over the frame, using thumbtacks or staples to secure the fabric on the back. Start at the center of each side, stapling one side and then its opposite, slowly working your way out to the corners. This stretches the fabric taut, and enables the canvas to develop an even tension. Work the design exactly as you would on an embroidery hoop.

If you have worked successfully all your life without using a frame, it will probably be very frustrating to start using one. Some people complain that it is annoying to take a frame around with them: they love to just pick up and carry a piece of needlepoint anywhere. The solution to this is, do all the complicated shading at home on the frame and fill in the background in your hand wherever you happen to be.

Alternatively, the portable hoop on a lap stand was specially designed for the traveling needlepointer. If you are first starting out, you will find that using a frame is a good habit to establish right away.

THREADING THE NEEDLE

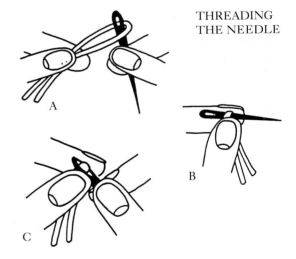

THREADING
THE NEEDLE

A. Wrap the thread around the needle as shown.

B. Hold the thread tightly close around the needle, and pull the needle away.

C. Squeeze the thread *tightly* between your finger and thumb, so that the thread is almost buried. Press eye of the needle flat down on the thread, rather than trying to attempt to push the thread through the needle. Pull through when the amount of thread shown in the diagram has appeared.

THE BASIC STITCH

Note: To learn the basic stitch, take a scrap of canvas or work on the waste canvas at the edge of the design. Secure the thread and bring your needle up anywhere on the front of the canvas. Use the point of your needle to count *one thread* immediately *above* where your thread came out one thread over to the right. Go down through the canvas. You have now completed one stitch.

Slanting from left to right, the stitch covers one intersection of the canvas. All of the other stitches will be *exactly the same*. Bring the needle up anywhere on the canvas, and complete another stitch.

Once you have worked several of these scattered stitches, check to see that they all slant in the same direction—the stitch is always identical wherever you work on the canvas. You are now ready to work the stitches in rows, horizontally or vertically, or diagonally as shown on pages 121 and 122. Continue to see each stitch as an individual stitch, even when it is fitted side by side with another.

STARTING AND ENDING OFF

To Begin Stitching:

Decide the amount of thread (what ply) and needle size you will need for the mesh (see chart p. 126). Thread your needle, put a knot in the end of the yarn, and go down from the top through the canvas about one inch away from where you are about to begin stitching. Come up where you plan to begin working, and as you stitch towards the knot, you will automatically cover the thread which lies on the back. When your stitching comes close to the knot, simply cut off the knot on the front of the canvas, as by now, the thread lying on the reverse side will have been secured by stitches.

To End Off Stitching:

End off in the same way as you began. Leave the end of the thread hanging on the front of the work, one inch away from your last stitches. As soon as the yarn lying on the back is covered, cut off the remaining amount on the front of the canvas.

TO BEGIN STITCHING

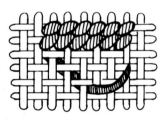

TO END OFF STITCHING

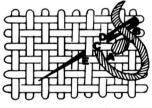

FIG. 1
TENT STITCH
WORKED HORI-
ZONTALLY

FIG. 2
TENT STITCH
WORKED HORI-
ZONTALLY

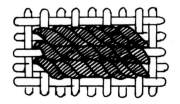

FIG. 3
TENT STITCH
SHOWING
REVERSE SIDE
WORKED HORI-
ZONTALLY

THE STITCHES

The most universal stitch used for needlepoint is called the tent stitch. The tent stitch slants across each intersection of the canvas, covering the mesh completely. The smooth result gives the effect of woven tapestry, and it is extremely durable. The size of the stitch depends on the number of threads per square inch of your canvas mesh. This can be very fine, ranging from twenty-six, twenty-two, or eighteen threads to the inch (known as petit point), to sixteen, fourteen, twelve, or ten (sometimes called demi-point), to seven or five (known as gros point).

The cross stitch is an alternative needlepoint stitch, excellent for rugs because of its bold effect and hard-wearing qualities. The slanted tent stitch is crossed over with a stitch going in the opposite direction, forming an X. Because of this double stitching, it does take a little longer to work and almost twice the yarn.

TENT STITCH (CONTINENTAL STITCH)

Tent stitch, the basic stitch used for needlepoint, has long slanting stitches covering the canvas, on the reverse side. If you have never tried needlepoint before, you may find the note on The Basic Stitch helpful before you begin.

FIG. 4   FIG. 5
TENT STITCH WORKED VERTICALLY

Worked Horizontally (see figs. 1–3)

When the tent stitch is worked in straight lines (horizontally or vertically), it is often called the continental stitch. Start in at the lower right of the area to be filled, come up at A. Go down at B (one thread above and one thread to the right of A). Come up at C, one thread to the left, and level with A. Repeat, going in at D, up at E, making a horizontal row of slanting stitches, working from right to left across the canvas.

At the end of the line, turn the canvas and work a second row of identical stitches above the first. Bring the needle up in the same holes as the previous line of stitches, so that no canvas shows between. By turning the canvas completely around at the end of each line, the rows are always worked from right to left, making it easier for those who are right-handed to "sew" each stitch with the needle slanted as in the diagram. Left-handed people should simply turn these diagrams upside down to follow them, beginning each area to be filled at the top left-hand corner. For effect on the reverse side see diagram.

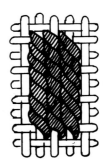

FIG. 6
TENT STITCH
SHOWING
REVERSE SIDE
WORKED
VERTICALLY

Worked Vertically (see figs. 4–6)

The tent stitch may also be worked in vertical rows, turning the canvas so that you always work from top to bottom. Begin at the top left of the area to be filled.

FIG. 7
TENT
STITCH
WORKED
DIAGONALLY

BASKET WEAVE (TENT STITCH WORKED DIAGONALLY)

Worked Diagonally (see figs. 7–11)

The tent stitch may also be worked diagonally known as basket weave (see figs. 7 and 8). When working from the top to bottom, the needle is placed vertically so that the next stitch may be taken on the true diagonal of the mesh.

When working from bottom to top, the needle is horizontal. This gives a basket weave effect on the back which is durable and firm. The stitch is clear-cut because the needle always goes down into the previous stitches, never up. The canvas does not have to be reversed at the end of each row as in the continental stitch. This makes it practical for filling in the backgrounds. To learn the stitch, practice it as shown in the diagrams on an odd bit of canvas. Once it is understood that it is identical with hor-

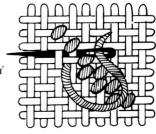

FIG. 8
TENT
STITCH
WORKED
DIAGONALLY

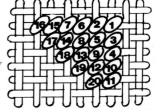

FIG. 9
TENT
STITCH
WORKED
DIAGONALLY

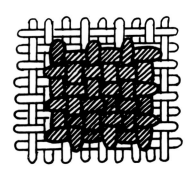

FIG. 10
TENT STITCH
SHOWING
REVERSE SIDE

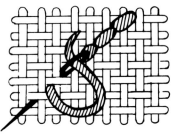

FIG. 11
TENT STITCH
SLANTING

izontal and vertical tent stitch only worked diagonally, it will be easy to work a corner following fig. 9.

Begin in the top right-hand corner, and always work the rows alternately—first from top to bottom, and then from bottom to top, starting with one stitch, and increasing each row as shown. Always leave a thread hanging in the middle of the row if you have to leave the canvas, then when you pick it up again you can tell whether you were working up or down the canvas. When two rows are worked in the same direction the basket weave on the back is interrupted; this makes an undesirable break which shows on the front. Reverse side, showing basket weave, see fig. 10.

Sometimes it is necessary to work diagonal lines of tent stitch slanting from left to right as shown in fig. 11. In this case, the stitch becomes like a back stitch. The needle comes up one thread to the left and one thread below the last stitch, and goes down into the exact same hole as this previous stitch, as shown. A whole background of lines in this direction would not be smooth, as the stitches do not interlock.

CROSS STITCH (figs. 12–14)

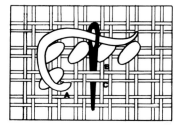

FIG. 12
CROSS STITCH

Cross stitch is very durable and is therefore an excellent stitch for working rugs. Working on a large mesh canvas for rugs, Penelope canvas is often used for its durability. Cross stitch can also be worked on mono and interlock canvases.

On Penelope Canvas

fig. 12 Come up at A, count one double thread up and one double thread over to the right, and go in at B. Come up at C, one thread immediately below B. The needle is therefore always vertical, as shown. Work to the end of the line.

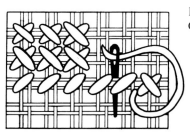

FIG. 13
CROSS STITCH

fig. 13 Complete the cross by working back in the opposite direction, going into exactly the same holes as the previous stitches, as shown.

fig. 14 This shows the small upright stitches formed on the reverse side.

On Mono Canvas

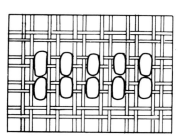

FIG. 14
CROSS STITCH
SHOWING
REVERSE SIDE

Cross stitch can also be worked on Mono canvas. The first stitch is taken with the needle placed vertically. The second is crossed over, with the needle slanting as in the tent stitch, making a long stitch on the wrong side. This makes a firmer stitch because it pulls against the weave of the Mono canvas. It also wears better although it does use more wool.

STRETCHING AND BLOCKING

Before mounting any finished needlepoint, the canvas should be blocked. First buy four artists' stretcher strips that are large enough to surround the design yet are not too big that you cannot overlap at least one inch of canvas over the wooden strips for stretching.

Assemble the stretchers to form a square. Mark the center point on each of the four stretchers. Fold the canvas and mark the center point on each of the four sides of the needlepoint. Align these marks on the canvas and stretchers, and with a heavy-duty staple gun, attach the needlepoint to the stretchers on all edges. First staple the center of one side, then pull the needlepoint out with pliers to staple the opposite side. Work around each side, starting at the center of each side and working out to the corners, stapling one side against the other until the work is stretched really tight and square.

With a sponge and cold water, soak the needlepoint and allow it to dry in its own time—you can even run the cold tap of the bathtub through the needlepoint and allow it to stand in the tub until dry. (It may be wise to test for color fastness before doing this.)

When it has dried thoroughly, remove the staples, and if it is not being mounted immediately, roll it around a cardboard tube, right side outward.

MOUNTING PILLOWS, RUGS, AND PICTURES

Once the finished piece has been blocked, it is ready for mounting. Because needlepoint is so hard wearing it is excellent for making up into rugs, chair seats, wall hangings, and pillows, as well as things to wear such as belts, slippers, handbags, and vests. A basic outline for pillow making, rug finishing, and picture framing is given here. For all other projects, professional upholstery and finishing is highly recommended. Your finished masterpiece deserves the care and expertise only an experienced professional can give.

Pillows

The two basic pillow finishes are the "knife edge" and the "box." For a knife-edged pillow, the front and back are sewn together with only a narrow piping to divide them. For a box pillow, a fabric strip is sewn to form a band between the front and back, creating the box effect. Either of these shapes can be further enhanced by adding cords, looped fringes, piping, or tassels.

To make a knife-edged pillow, take the finished, blocked needlepoint and trim away the unworked canvas all around to a half-inch margin. If you are adding cording it will be sewn on afterwards, but if you are adding piping, fringe, or a cord with a flange, pin it to the right side of the needlework along the seam line, raw edges outward, basting it in place along the edge of the stitching. It is a good idea to overlap the needlepoint stitching by one or two threads, so no white canvas will show around the edge of the finished pillow. Also, at each corner, instead of basting the fringe at a sharp angle, baste it in a curve. This will make it easier to get the stuffing right up into the corners of the pillow later, and will avoid unattractive points at the four corners known as "rabbit ears."

Next, cut the backing the same size as the front and then lay the needlepoint face down on the backing, with right sides facing. Baste backing and needlepoint together, starting at the center of each side, then stitch by machine through all the thicknesses. Be sure to leave a half-inch seam allowance and a six-inch opening at the lower right-hand corner. Trim the corners and excess margin and make tiny snips into the turn-backs at the corners and curves.

Now, make a knife-edged pillow form in muslin, one inch larger than the needlepoint pillow. (Pillow forms can be purchased at many supply shops in all shapes and sizes.) To make the form, cut two pieces of muslin, leaving a half-inch seam allowance all around. Sew together, leaving a four-inch opening, turn right side out and then fill with down or fiber fill. Sew the opening closed. Gently stuff this liner into the needlepoint pillow, and carefully and invisibly sew up the opening at the lower right.

To make a boxed pillow, follow the same procedures, laying the boxing strip down on top of the pillow front with the fringe or piping basted in place. Baste and machine stitch all the way around. Sew the edges of the boxing together where they meet, using a half-inch seam. Then, sew the backing to the boxing, right side facing, leaving a six-inch opening. Proceed as in the knife-edge pillow, making or purchasing a boxed pillow form large enough to fit the pillow, and maintain a firm shape when the pillow is stuffed. Sew the opening closed.

Cords may be stitched around the edges afterwards using a long slanting stitch which slides between the twists of the cord and becomes invisible. Some tassels require stitching in place afterwards, others may be fastened on as you stitch the fringe in place.

Rugs

To maintain the rug's even shape, spray the back of the rug with spray starch while it is being blocked. Lay the blocked rug face down on an ironing board. Press back the canvas edges all around, using a steam iron and making sure no unworked canvas shows in front. Trim the turn-backs to within one inch all around. On a curved rug snip vertically into the turn-backs every few inches to allow the canvas to lie flat around the curves. On a square rug cut off a triangular piece at each corner of the canvas, leaving half an inch of unworked canvas between the slice and the needlepoint. Fold over this remaining half-inch turn-back, then fold in the two sides and stitch the two straight edges together. They will form a miter that makes a flat corner. Repeat this for the remaining three corners, and baste all four straight edges down. Cut the backing to the same size as the finished needlepoint plus a half-inch for the turn-backs. Attach backing to the reverse side of the rug by basting diagonally from corner to corner (to prevent slipping). Turn under the backing's edges and hem the backing to the rug all around. Start stitching from the center of each side and work out to the corners to maintain even placement.

Note: When choosing backing fabric, choose a linen weave or any porous material which will allow the dirt to pass through. Otherwise, dirt will be trapped between the needlepoint and the backing which will cut the stitches.

Pictures

To prepare a needlepoint to hang on the wall, either frame it within a regular picture frame or mount it on a composite or fiber board. Because needlepoint resembles tapestry, the softness of the wool is shown best without glass over it. Glass tends to compress the stitches and reflect the light, so it is preferable to do without it. To make a framed picture, buy four frame pieces to fit the design (available at art supply stores), and after blocking the work leave it on the stretcher strips. Now just fit the pieces around the stretched needlepoint and assemble the frame. Use two eye screws and picture-hanging wire at the back of the work to hang it. These should be screwed into the stretchers and not into the frame.

If you prefer to hang up the needlepoint without a frame, simply remove your canvas from the stretcher strips. Purchase a piece of composite or fiber board a half-inch smaller than the finished design, and some cotton sheeting and batting approximately the same size as the entire canvas. First attach the batting evenly on the board, holding it in place with wide masking tape. Next, cover it with cotton attached in the same manner. Then, placing the needlepoint face down on a flat surface, put the cotton-covered board over it. Place it so that only the design will be exposed on the right side and no raw canvas shows. Tack down the four edges with tape, working opposite sides against one another as in blocking (see p. 123). Once the work has been evenly placed, the four edges can be stapled to the board with a staple gun. Cut backing fabric ½" larger than the finished picture; press these ½" turnbacks down and secure by hemming all around as described in *Rugs* above.

Now two eye screws can be attached and wire strung between— creating a simple mounted picture. Here, nothing competes with the beauty of the needlework.

Starting Out

Beginners: If you are starting needlepoint for the first time, pick a small project that will give you an encouraging sense of achievement. Your stitching will inevitably become smooth and even with practice!

Color sorting: Separate the yarn colors into groups. Then knot all the shades of blue, all the browns, all the greens together, for instance. By looping a thread around each bundle, and pulling tight, you can easily pull one thread out at a time from the bundle.

Canvas fraying: Bind the edges of your canvas with masking or white artists' tape to avoid fraying and irritating rough edges. You may also machine stitch an overlock line around the edges to prevent fraying.

Stitching

Stitch direction: Always mark the canvas TOP. Then your stitches will always slant in the correct direction. It is easy to turn the work sideways and find you have worked the stitches on the wrong slant!

Tension: Be sure stitches are even and clear. If your yarn is too heavy and your stitches are loose, the finished needlepoint will feel very stiff and the result may look lumpy. If, on the other hand, the threads are too thin and you pull tightly, you will not cover the canvas and your work will look worn.

Yarn twisting: Yarns tend to twist while stitching. To cure this, allow the needle to dangle from the canvas and smooth the yarn with your fingers to untwist it.

Unpicking: To unpick your work if you have made a mistake, cut all the long stitches on the reverse side with a pair of sharp scissors, being careful not to cut the canvas. Turn to the right side, and cut again. Try to rough up the stitches again on the front by rubbing with the flat point of the scissors. You may remove loose snippets with a pair of tweezers.

Finishing

Missed stitches: Check your work after it has been blocked for any missed stitches by holding it up to a light.

CANVAS, YARN USAGE, AND NEEDLE CHART

Canvas Mesh Size	Erica Wilson 3 Strand Persian Wool	DMC 6 Strand Cotton Floss	DMC Single Strand Cotton Perle	Needle Size
18	1 Strand	4–6 Strands	1 Strand No. 5	24
16	1 Strand	6 Strands	1 Strand No. 5	22
14	1 Strand	6–8 Strands	1 Strand No. 3	20
12	2 Strands	9 Strands	1 Strand No. 3	18–20
10	3 Strands	12 Strands	—	18
7	6 Strands	—	—	16

COLOR COMPARISON CHART

(All numbers represent the closest equivalent shade.)

E. W. PERSIAN	PATERNAYAN	DMC FLOSS	ANCHOR WOOL
WHITES:			
1001	260	SNOW WHITE	800
1010	262	ECRU	8006
1012	263	712	8032
1017	246	3072	9782
BLACKS:			
1050	220	310	9800
1051	221	844	9798
GRAYS:			
1061	200	413 OR 645	9764
1062	201	414 OR 317	8876
1064	203	415 OR 647	8892
1071-1074	210-213	-	8720,8712,8596,8602,8582
1091-1094	-	-	-
BROWNS:			
1106	405	-	9508
1111	410	632	9646
1113	412	434	8064
1122	421	3371	9666
1124	423	433	9452
1142	441	420	9408
1143	442	-	9388
1144	443	422	9404
1145	444	738	9324
1153-1156	452-455	610-613	-
1162	461	640	9662
1172	471	-	9624
1186	485	3064	9512
1201-1244	-	-	9664,9312,9306
REDS:			
2006	905	962	8522
2013	912	3687	8418
2015	914	3688	8504
2021	920	-	8428
2031	930	3350	8240
2032	931	3328	8348
2033	932	760	8368
2034	933	761	8366
2035	934	-	8364
2044	943	-	8438
2046	945	957	8432
2047	946	818	8394
2048	947	819	8392
2049	948	-	8342
2051	950	326	8442
2052	951	309	8204
2053	952	355	8440
2055	954	3706 OR 893	8396
2061	960	601	8456
2064	963	604	8452
2072	971	321	8200
2101-2104	-	-	8402,8416,8412,8498
ORANGES:			
3001	800	971	8156
3004	803	-	8138
3005	804	945	8132
3006	805	-	8296
3025	824	-	8152
3026	825	948	8352
3034	833	-	8234
3036	835	-	8254
3041	840	817	8218
3043	842	350	8198
3044	843	351	8196
3045	844	352	8258
3046	845	353	8304
3055	854	-	8232
3056	855	-	8302
3062	861	919	8162
3066	865	-	-
3071	870	355	8330
3075	874	-	8322
3085	884	-	9556
3091	-	975	9526
YELLOWS:			
4001	700	782	8140
4004	703	743	8136
4005	704	745	8132
4012	711	-	8022
4014	713	-	8016
4015	714	3078	8014
4016	715	-	8012
4017	716	746	8006
4023	722	976	9526
4025	724	977	8060
4026	725	-	8058
4028	727	744	8018
4031	730	780	8106
4032	731	781	8104
4033	732	-	8102
4034	733	-	8022
4035	734	-	8040
4036	735	-	8054
4043	742	-	8042
4046	745	3047	8024

E. W. PERSIAN	PATERNAYAN	DMC FLOSS	ANCHOR WOOL
4052	751	-	8044
4054	753	676	8060
4055	754	676	8052
4056	755	677	8036
4057	756	822	8034
4063	762	-	8112
4072	771	973	8120
GREENS:			
5004	603	3052	9076
5005	604	3053	9074
5006	605	-	9072
5011	610	319	9104
5013	612	320	9102
5014	613	368	9096
5015	614	369	9092
5021	620	909	9104
5022	621	911	9102
5023	622	954	9098
5025	624	-	9092
5032	631	904	9118
5033	632	905	9116
5035	634	907	9114
5036	635	-	9112
5044	643	3012	9310
5045	644	3013	9304
5052	651	936	9218
5053	652	-	9216
5054	653	733	9214
5061	660	935	9028
5062	661	-	9024
5063	662	-	9022
5064	663	-	9004
5065	664	-	9002
5066	665	-	9014
5067	666	-	9012
5071	670	580	9274
5073	672	3348	9282
5081	680	991	8942
5082	681	910	8990
5088	687	-	8984
5091	690	890	9208
5092	691	937	9204
5093	692	3346 OR 469	9156
5095	694	472	9194
5123	-	988	8986
5131	-	500	8884
5132	-	501	8880
5133	-	502	8876
5134	-	503	8874
5135	-	504	9012
PURPLES:			
6005	304	-	6524
6011	310	550	8530
6013	312	-	8592
6022	321	327	8528
6025	324	-	8522
6026	325	-	8482
6027	326	-	8542
6032	331	-	8590
BLUES:			
7002	501	311	8794
7003	502	312	8792
7004	503	322	8790
7005	504	334	8798
7006	505	3325	8796
7007	506	775	8794
7008	507	-	8792
7011	510	-	8740
7013	512	-	8738
7014	513	931	8734
7021	520	924	8884
7022	521	501	8902
7024	523	503	8876
7025	524	504	8874
7026	525	504	8872
7033	532	924	8882
7046	545	809	8686
7052	551	-	8690
7053	552	-	8688
7054	553	-	8672
7056	555	-	8684
7065	564	-	8786
7072	571	-	8694
7086	585	747	8802
7092	591	806	8894
7093	592	-	8808
7094	593	807	8806
7095	594	-	8804
7096	595	598	8802
7101-7103	-	-	8744,8794,8790
7111	-	-	8674
7112	-	995	8688
7121	-	791	8694
7124	-	794	8776
7131	-	939	8638
7132	-	-	8636

RESOURCES

For information about Erica Wilson's needlework kits for The Metropolitan Museum of Art, please contact:

Special Service Office
The Metropolitan Museum of Art
Middle Village, NY 11381-0001

Erica Wilson Needle Works
717 Madison Avenue
New York, NY 10021
(212) 832-7290
and
Erica Wilson Needle Works
25 Main Street
Nantucket, MA 02554
(508) 228-9881

Coats Crafts UK
P.O. Box 22
McMullen Road
Darlington
Co. Durham DL1 1YO
01325 381010
UK

Priscilla's Tapestry
1205 High Street
Malvern
Victoria 3144
Australia
3 982 25131

Erica Wilson Needle Works can also supply Erica Wilson Persian Yarn, Paternayan Yarn, Appleton Yarn, DMC thread, canvas by the yard, needles, Trace Erase pens, cords and tassels, pillow mounting, and upholstery.

Manufacturers who can supply you with your nearest retailer:

DMC YARNS:

DMC Corporation
Port Kearny
Building 10
South Kearny, NJ 07032
(201) 589-0606
USA

DMC Creative World Ltd
Pullman Road
Wigston
Leicester LE8 2DY
UK
01533 811040

DMC Needlecraft Pty Ltd.
51-56 Carrington Road
Marrick Ville
NSW 2204
Australia
2 559 3088

CANVAS AND RUG BACKING:

Joan Toggitt Ltd.; Zweigart Ltd.
Weston Canal Plaza
2 Riverview Drive
Somerset, NJ 08873
(908) 271-1949
USA

For stretching and backing needlepoint services inquire at needlework or furnishing fabric shops.

CORDS AND TASSELS:

D'Kei
P.O. Box 450
1108 Front Street
Lisle, IL 60532
(708) 963-2093
(800) 535-3534
USA

Peter Jones
Sloane Square
London SW1
UK
0171 730 3434

V.V. Rouleaux
201 New Kings Road
London SW6
UK
0171 371 5929

De Winter Ltd.
223 Kensington Church Street
London W8 7LX
UK
0171 229 4949

PILLOW STUFFING:

Fairfield Processing Corp.
88 Rose Hill Avenue
Danbury, CT 06813-1157
(203) 744-2090
(800) 243-0989
USA

SILK AND METALLIC THREADS:

Kreinick Manufacturing
P.O. Box 1966
Parkersburg, WV 26102
(304) 422-8900
(800) 624-1428
USA

Coats Crafts UK
P.O. Box 22
McMullen Road
Darlington
Co. Durham DL1 1YO
01325 381010
for Kreinick threads

DMC Creative World Ltd
Pullman Road
Wigston
Leicester LE8 2DY
UK
01533 811041

Chipping Camden Needlecraft Centre
High Street
Chipping Camden
Gloucestershire
UK
01386 840583

Coats Paton Crafts
89-91 Peters Avenue
Mulgrave
Victoria 3170
Australia